Some of the participants...

Mary Fryer    married 1820    William Green, Esq.

and their daughter,
Nancy Judith Green,
m. Oct. 20, 1857,
James H. Bryan(t).

# White County, Tennessee
# OLDEST MARRIAGE BOOK
## 1809 - 1859

*Copied by*
Mary Fancher Mitchell

*Arranged by*
J. Sharon Johnson Doliante

CLEARFIELD

# INTRODUCTION

WHITE COUNTY, TENNESSEE was formed by an Act of the General Assembly, meeting in Knoxville, on Sept. 11, 1806, after a petition requesting that such a county be formed was drawn up and signed by approximately 155 residents, including John White (Sr.), Woodson P. White, and John Scoggin (Jr.). John White was the father and father-in-law, respectively, of the last two. These men were then living in what is now the northern or north central portion of White County, and appear to have been well settled there for some months, according to Charles Leonard, of Sparta (1976), who located this historic petition (#5-1-1806), at the Tennessee State Library and Archives, in Nashville. The petition itself bore no date, but an attached sheet contained the date, July 22, 1806. The endorsement was to Mr. Chisum and Sampson Williams, who were in Jackson County, in 1802.

THE TENNESSEE STATE LIBRARY AND ARCHIVES states flatly and without equivocation, that White County was named for this same John White. So too, have county historians, past and present, and state erected highway signs proclaim the same, at the county boundaries. In GENEALOGICAL SERENDIPITY, Vol. I, published in 1965, and which included data on the White and Scoggin families, we voiced doubt that the county actually was named for John White, as we proved he was not in the area nearly so early as historians have claimed.

JOHN WHITE, SR., a veteran of the Revolutionary War, and a native of Amelia County, Virginia, sold land he owned in Washington County, Virginia, on October 18, 1805, and together with his family (including son-in-law, John Scoggin, Jr.), moved into middle Tennessee. It's entirely possible, and even probable, that these men had previously explored the region they chose for their new home.

IN THE LIGHT of the discovery by Charles Leonard of the petition of 1806, we are now inclined to give some credence to the possibility that the county may indeed have been named for John White, Sr. In his will dated White County, 1843, and proved there in 1846, John White mentioned that he had given to his son Woodson, "in his lifetime, one set of surveying instruments", leading one to the conclusion that both men were surveyors...and quite possibly responsible for laying out or helping to lay out the original boundary lines for the county. In all fairness though, we must report that Charles Leonard has not changed the opinion he has long held, that the county was named for James White, founder of Knoxville, and father of Hugh Lawson White, one of the wealthiest and most influential men of his day, in the then fledgling state of Tennessee.

ALTHOUGH our friend Charles reports that John White still has descendants who live in the northern portion of White County, in the area where John, Sr. originally lived, this early settler bought 592 acres of land in southern White County, on June 1, 1808, and built his home there (it is labeled by county historians, the "oldest house in White County"), in what is known as Hickory Valley, and his son-in-law, John Scoggin, Jr., settled near him, in the area now known as Doyle, on his first land, a state grant of 144 acres, issued September 26, 1808.

WHITE COUNTY originally encompassed all of what is now Warren County, as well as parts of the counties of Cannon, Coffee, De Kalb, Franklin, Grundy, Putnam, and Van Buren.

ABOUT a quarter of a century ago, the late Mrs. B. K. Mitchell, nee Mary Fancher, served White County as Clerk and Master, and continued in this capacity or in that of Deputy Clerk and Master, off and on for the next 10 or 15 years. During this period she copied many of the oldest marriage records, including some loose sheets in the old dirt-floored basement vault of the courthouse. We first met her about 1961, while visiting in Sparta to gather material for GENEALOGICAL SERENDIPITY, Vol. I. Some time later, Charles Leonard, to whom she had given her copy of the marriage records, allowed us to make a copy. We wanted to publish them then, but since they ended at such an odd period...February 1, 1859, we urged Mrs. Mitchell to bring them up through at least 1860, and preferably 1880. This she promised to do, but she never did tell us that she had done so.

YEARS WENT BY, and we forgot all about the old records which Mrs. Mitchell had titled, "Oldest Marriage Book". This past summer we came across them again, and decided to go ahead and publish them, brief though the record is. We typed the manuscript, and were about ready for publication, when we again had occasion to communicate with Charles Leonard, from whom we had not heard in several years. He reported to us that Mrs. Mitchell had, before her decease, completed the "Oldest Marriage Book", (we thought it was complete in our records!), and that it ran into the 1880's, or thereabouts! And, Mrs. Mitchell had left her records to Charles. He expressed much pleasure that we were about to publish the records we had, but we now found ourself with a typed and completed manuscript, entitled "Oldest Marriage Book...", while in fact it is only approximately half of the oldest marriage book! Nevertheless, we have elected to present what records we have, and hope that Charles will one day publish the other half!

THE EARLIEST MARRIAGE Mrs. Mitchell located is dated Dec. 4, 1809, and was between John Puckett and Rhody Lyda. This record and 32 others, Mrs. Mitchell followed by the letters, "L. P.-B. V.", which translates to: "Loose Page-Basement Vault". Charles now tells us that while Mrs. Mitchell carefully returned these papers to the vault all those years ago, they are now missing! He further relates that there is no longer a basement vault (or, at least not the one Mrs. Mitchell referred to), as Sparta now boasts a new courthouse. So this may well be the only permanent record of those early marriages.

IT SEEMED to this compiler that many early marriage records must be missing from White County records, but only pages "1" and "20" are missing from the old marriage book, which is apparently complete (with these exceptions), for all the marriage licenses issued during the period covered. We trust that our readers will not object to the fact that we included several marriages for members of our own families, for which we had reliable references, but which do not appear in courthouse records, for reasons we cannot fathom. The Bible records referred to are mentioned, or photocopies of them appear, in GENEALOGICAL SERENDIPITY, Vol. I. We now learn that Charles Leonard also has a handful of similar marriages which we would happily have included, had we but known of them in time.

THERE ARE only two marriages herein, between black or "colored" persons, the reason presumably being that all of these marriages occurred before the Civil War and slaves were not allowed to marry. Both are clearly labeled. Incidentally, the term "colored" indicates mixed blood, and might as easily refer to Indians, as blacks. After the groom's name on one of these, appear the letters, "F.M.C." (free man of color); and after his bride's name, "F. W. C." (free woman of color).

WE WISH to point out to our readers the frequency with which some of the families intermarried. Often, it seems, several brothers &/or sisters of one family, married sisters &/or brothers of another family.

CHARLES LEONARD, who is an historian as well as a genealogist (and a former librarian for the National Genealogical Society Library, Washington, D. C.), supplied all of the incidental information concerning the early White County ministers. The reader will note that several of these seem to have performed only one, or a very few marriages...although it must be noted that there are many marriages for whom no minister or justice is named. Some were undoubtedly itinerant, but the tombstone of our ancestor, Rev. John Greene, who is buried on his own land in Lost Creek, White County, states: "John Greene/Born/Mar. 24, 1777/ Died/Mar. 30, 1853/A Baptist Minister for 43 years..." He purchased his first land in White County, Aug. 10, 1810, so he spent the entire 43 years of his ministry in White County, and yet there are only 5 marriages on record, which he is credited with performing. And our ancestor, Rev. John Scoggin, Jr., was a Methodist minister and lived in White County for over 50 years, yet there are no marriages of record which he performed, both of which facts seem incredible.

WE FEEL compelled to mention that as a native of Arkansas, we recognized a fairly large number of rather unusual surnames among these marriages, which we have never heard anywhere else, except in the Arkansas school systems, 30 or 40 years ago, especially in the Little Rock schools; therefore we suspect that many of the early White Countians migrated to Arkansas, where there are still, no doubt, many descendants. And while we assure our readers that we made every effort to eliminate errors from these records, it would be unusual if some had not crept in. Therefore, if a reader discovers the marriage of his ancestors herein, we urge that he attempt to secure a photocopy or certified copy from the Clerk and Master, White County, Sparta, Tennessee 38583. Also, do search for all possible spellings herein, for the name sought. We have left them exactly as we found them, mis-spellings and all!

OUR THANKS to Charles Leonard for his help, past and present. He has always been most generous in sharing his knowledge of White County and White Countians. And special thanks to William John Doliante, husband extraordinaire, who so patiently helped us proof-read these pages. We couldn't have managed without him.


Mrs. Wm. J. Doliante
380 Sheffield Drive
Santa Barbara, Ca. 93108
November, 1976

vii.

\_\_\_\_\_, \_\_\_\_\_ & Agatha Howel-(not returned)-Dec. 9, 1841-p. 10

ABBOTT, Wm. M. & Martha L. Ingalls-May 13, 1854, by J. C. Stephens, Esq.-p. 48

ACTKINSON, Jas. W. & Elizabeth Anderson-Oct. 25, 1855-p. 51

ADCOCK, Isaac & Miss Mary Ann Davis-Dec. 17, 1845, by Thos. Jones, Esq.-p. 21

ADCOCK, James & Zeda Quillen-Feb. 11, 1852, by Wm. I. Russell, Esq.-p. 40

ADCOCK, Leonard & Rachel Clouse-Oct. 28, 1842, by Thos. Jones, Esq.-p. 14

ADCOCK, Wm. & Martha Davis-Oct. 19, 1848, by A. L. Shaw, Esq.-p. 30

ADAIR, Lewis & Catharine Keithley-Dec. 23, 1840-p. 10

ADAIR, Pleasant & Mary R. Earles-Sept. 23, 1850, by E. W. Denton, Esq.-p. 35

ADAIR, Thos. & Margarett Adair-Apr. 24, 1851, by Creed A. Taylor, Esq.-p. 37

ADAIR, Wm. L. & Martha Brown-June 27, 1840, by Rev. James Simmons-p. 9

ADIER, James & Malissa E. Carroll-Feb. 16, 1847-p. 25

ADKINS, Jacob & Charlotte Cunningham-July 14, 1843, by Elijah W. Denton, Esq.-p.15

ALBY, Howard & Eliza Jane Netherton-Dec. 12, 1858, by Richard Bradley, Esq.-p. 59

ALEXANDER, Geo. W. & Mary Cox-Feb. 28, 1850, by Joseph S. Menefee, Esq.-p. 34

ALLBRIGHT, Wm. M. & Elizabeth Moore-Oct. 21, 1849, by Rev. John Julien-p. 32

ALLEN, James & Martha Jane Wilson-Dec. 11, 1851-p. 39

ALLEN, James M. & Mary Jane Lollar-Oct. 19, 1851, by Robt. Hitchcock-p. 39

ALLEN, John W. & Mary Ann Watson-Nov. 13, 1849, by Rev. Thos. Stone-p. 32

ALLEN, Joshua & Margarett Truett-Dec. 26, 1841, by Wm. R. Tucker, Esq.-p. 12

ALLISON, James S. & Rachel E. Clark-July 30, 1846, by Rev. Levi Perkins-p. 23

ALLISON, William H. & Elizabeth P. Clark-Aug. 23, 1846, by Rev. Levi Perkins-p.23

ALVERSON, James M. & Martha J. Green-Sept. 15, 1856, by C. A. Taylor, Esq.-p. 54

ALVERSON, Thos. J. & Martha J. Kerr-Jan. 2, 1851, by Rev. J. H. Morgan-p. 36

ANDERSON, Allen & Elizabeth Smith-Jan. 24, 1856, by Henry J. Lyda, Esq.-p. 52

ANDERSON, Archibald C. & Mary J. Robbins-Feb. 16, 1857-p. 55

ANDERSON, Charles & Nancy Whitley-Dec. 22, 1842, by Robt. H. McManus, Esq.-p. 14

ANDERSON, Charles & Mrs. Caroline Baker-Jan. 19, 1859, by Rev. John M. Lansden-p. 59

ANDERSON, Edward & Sarah Glenn-Aug. 5, 1857, by Alexander Oliver, Esq.-p. 56

ANDERSON, James & Nancy De Freese-(not returned)-Apr. 29, 1841-p. 11

ANDERSON, James & Emily Clenny-Oct. 3, 1843-p. 16

ANDERSON, James & Jane Welch-Aug. 8, 1844, by Joseph G. Mitchell, Esq.-p. 18

ANDERSON, Jasper N. & Caroline Weaver-Dec. 22, 1845-p. 19

ANDERSON, John & Minney Adair-Dec. 30, 1818-(L.P.-B.V.)

ANDERSON, John & Helen M. Bradshaw-Jan. 29, 1849, by J. H. Morgan-p. 31

ANDERSON, John D. & Mary Denton-Oct. 29, 1840, by Rev. James H. Morgan-p. 9

ANDERSON, John L. & Nancy Short-Jan. 29, 1850-p. 33

ANDERSON, Joseph M. & Sarah Denton-Jan. 28, 1841, by Matthias Hutson, Esq.-p. 10

ANDERSON, Marion & Rachel Blalock-Mar. 19, 1848, by D. Snodgrass, Esq.-p. 28

ANDERSON, Nathan & Evaline Green-Mar. 12, 1852, by Rev. James Herd-p. 40

ANDERSON, Robt. H. & Mahala McBride-Aug. 24, 1851, by W. L. Woods, Esq.-p. 38

ANDERSON, Spencer & Luzana Heifner-Mar. 10, 1853-p. 44

ANDERSON, Thos. J. & Charlotte Little-Dec. 11, 1856, by Rev. Isaac Denton-p. 54

ANDERSON, Wm. & Elizabeth Jackson-Jan. 5, 1849, by James Jackson, Esq.-p. 30

ANDERSON, Wm. & Mary White-Mar. 5, 1851-p. 37

ANDERSON, Wm. H. & Caroline E. Goodwin-Feb. 5, 1846, by Rev. James Herd-p. 22

ANDERSON, Wm. M. & Nancy A. Little-Feb. 22, 1849, by Rev. R. A. Forest-p. 31

ANDRUS, Laben & Charlotta Taylor-Mar. 31, 1844, by John Crook, Esq.-p. 17

APPLE, Sydney & Nancy Elms-Jan. 19, 1859, by Alvy Bussell, Esq.-p. 59

ARNOLD, Colbird & Lucinda Jane Whitley-Jan. 19, 1854, by Wm. Clayton, Esq.-p.47

ARNOLD, Columbus & Susan Pirtle-Jan. 5, 1858, by Joseph W. Clark, Esq.-p. 57

ARNOLD, Francis & Martha Ann Smith-Sept. 7, 1843, by Rev. Jesse E. Hickman-p. 16

ARNOLD, Napoleon B. & Sarah Milam-Mar. 16, 1858-p. 57

AUSTIN, James M. & Mary Anderson-Mar. 22, 1839, by Anderson S. Rogers-p. 4

AUSTIN, John, Jr. & Rebecca England-June 27, 1841, by Wm. Hudgens, Esq.-p. 12

AUSTIN, John, Senr. & Mary Ann Todd-Jan. 17, 1844-p. 17

AUSTIN, Nathan G. & Martha Jane Bryan-Jan. 21, 1847-p. 25. [Dau. of Wm.?]

AUSTIN, Pleasant & Mary E. Warren-Sept. 14, 1852, by M. Y. Brockett-p. 42

AUSTIN, Raleigh & Mary McDaniel-June 17, 1838, by John Bryan, Esq.-p. 2

AUSTIN, Robinson & Elizabeth England-Jan. 31, 1856, by Wm. Wilson, Esquire-p. 52

AUSTIN, Wm. E. & Mary Frasure-Jan. 24, 1859, by Wm. Clayton, Esq.-p. 59

AVERY, Henry & Elizabeth Green-Nov. 25, 1819-[Ref: A FRAGMENTARY GENEALOGICAL RE-
CORD...MYER AVERY and...PETER AVERY, by John H. Avery (Colo. Sprgs.,1914).]

BAILEY, James & Jane A. Bramlett-Nov. 2, 1843, by Rev. Jesse Hickman-p. 16

BAKER, Andrew & Mary Davis-Sept. 23, 1847, by Rev. Levi Perkins-p. 26

BAKER, Anthony & Levicey Howard-Jan. 15, 1846, by Alvey Bussell, Esq.-p. 21

BAKER, Dabney C.A. & Nancy Ann Kittrell-Mar. 22, 1848, by J.M. Sullivan, Esq.-p.28

BAKER, Green H. & Ann E. Taylor-May 8, 1839, by Asa Certain-p. 5

BAKER, Hezekiah & Eliza Ann Bray-Aug. 28, 1851, by Rev. M. W. McConnell-p. 38

BAKER, Jacob & Nancy Cole-Aug. 19, 1841, by Asa Certain, Esq.-p. 12

BAKER, Jacob & Elizabeth Blankenship-Oct. 11, 1853, by J. W. Glenn, Esq.-p. 46

BAKER, James & Rebecca Stacy-Sept. 17, 1843, by Wm. Austin, Esq.-p. 15

BAKER, James A. & Rebecca Ann Worley-Oct. 10, 1848-p. 30

BAKER, James M. & Elizabeth M. Simmons-Feb. 29, 1844, by Thos. Green, Esq.-p. 17

BAKER, John & Mary Frasur-Apr. 17, 1844-p. 17

BAKER, John & Eliza Dale-Nov. 23, 1853, by C. A. Taylor-p. 46

BAKER, John M. & Margaret Foster-NO DATE, but between Jan. 16 & 17, 1849-p. 30

BAKER, Johnathan & Margaret Linville-June 24, 1840, by Rev. J. E. Hickman-p. 9

-3-

BAKER, Jonathan & Minerva Cole-Jan. 27, 1842, by Thos. Jones, Esq.-p. 13

BAKER, Kile B. & Jane Suttle-Dec. 30, 1840, by Elijah Frost, Esq.-p. 7

BAKER, Matthias & Elizabeth J. Frost-Apr. 21, 1853, by Wm. Burden, M.G.-p. 44

BAKER, Meredith & Jane Kuhn-Dec. 21, 1854, by Rev. Aaron Deitz-p. 49

BAKER, Montgomery L. & Caroline Lowery-Feb. 28, 1850, by Wm. Clayton, Esq.-p. 34

BAKER, Reuben R. & Catharine Elvira White-Nov. 9, 1852, by Wm. Burden-p. 43

BAKER, Wm. & Mary Ann Wilhite-Sept. 1, 1840, by Rev. Josiah Williams-p. 9

BAKER, Wm. & Mary Elizabeth Whitmore-Apr. 24, 1851, by Creed A. Taylor, Esq.-p.37

BAKER, Wm. C. & Louisa Jenkins-Sept. 7, 1843, by Rev. Jesse E. Hickman-p. 16

BAKER, Wm. R. & Lucy C. Kerr-Dec. 22, 1853, by Rev. J. H. Morgan-p. 46

BALEW, Powell & Frances Parish-Feb. 26, 1850-p. 34

BALLEW, Joseph & Charlotte (?)Tolison-Aug. 18, 1855, by Alvy Bussell, Esq.-p. 51

BALLEW, Thos. & Sarah Tolison-Nov. 14, 1855, by Alva Bussell, Esq.-p. 52

BANDY, Thos. E. & Margaret O. Milican-Aug. 8, 1858, by John J. Duncan, Esq.-p.58

BARGAR, John & Mary Dunn-Dec. 20, 1849, by Robt. Hitchcock, Esq.-p. 33

BARGER, John & Sarah Wallis-May 25, 1851, by Wm. Clayton, Esq.-p. 37

BARNARD, Wm. & Sarah Smith-Jan. 28, 1858, by Richard Bradley, Esq.-p. 57

BARNES, Lewis T. & Mary Mills-Jan. 29, 1852, by Shadrach Price, Esq.-p. 40

BARNES, William & Nancy Jane Sailors-Jan. 29, 1846, by Rev. John B. Pointer-p.22

BARTLETT, Wm. & Arzella Robinson-Mar. 6, 1847-p. 25

BAYLY, Robert & Matilda Scoggins-Jan. 18, 1848, by David Snodgrass, Esq.-p. 27

BEAM, David & Elizabeth Dickinson-Sept. 7, 1850-p. 35

BEAN, Timothy & Mahulda Green-Feb. 14, 1855, by David Snodgrass-p. 50

BEATTY, John S. & Miss May Copland-Apr. 24, 1845-p. 19

BECK, James M. & Lamira Wilson-Dec. 23, 1854, by Rev. W. Burden-p. 49

BEDWELL, Leftwich & Rebecca Howard-Feb. 16, 1841, by John Pennington, Esq.-p.10

BELCHER, Bartlett & Malinda Fox-Mar. 22, 1848, by Thos. Cooper, Esq.-p. 28

BELL, John W. & Rachel Anderson-Nov. 18, 1845-p. 19

BENNETT, Alfred & Melissa Evans ('alias Webb')-May 30, 1858, by M.C. Dibrell, Esq.-p.58

BENNETT, Edward O. R. & Jane Tallent-Feb. 26, 1840, by Asa Certain, Esq.-p. 8

BENNETT, James H. & Mary E. Cope-Mar. 4, 1850, by Rev. James Herd-p. 34

BENNETT, Leonidas H. & Elizabeth E. Jones-Apr. 9, 1843, by Thos. Green, Esq.-p.15

BENNETT, Wm. H. & Susan Hitchcock-Oct. 9, 1856, by Alvey Bussell, Esq.-p. 54
[Is this a double wedding? See: John P. Manus.]

(?)BERRYMAN, Joseph A. & Celia Benton-Aug. 2, 1843-(not returned)-p. 15

BERTRAM, Wm. H. & Eleanor Taylor-May 21, 1850, by A. Graham, Esq.-p. 34

BINNINS, Calvin & Mary Rodgers-Feb. 27, 1847-p. 25

BLALOCK, John & Eliza Hampton-Feb. 15, 1846, by David Snodgrass, Esq.-p. 22

BLALOCK, McLen & Faney Jane Blalock-June 19, 1845, by Robt. Hitchcock, Esq.-p.19

BLALOCK, Michael & Mary Jane Corder-Aug. 1, 1853, by Elisha Scarboro-p. 45

BLANKENSHIP, Edmond & Nancy Holder-Oct. 25, 1848, by Rev. Thos. E. Hutson-p. 30

BLANKENSHIP, Granville & Tabitha Moss-June 11, 1849-p. 32

BLANKENSHIP, J.B.W. & Amanda Chisom-June 2, 1858, by John A. Templeton, Esq.-p.58

BLANKENSHIP, James & Nancy V. Rogers-Feb. 27, 1848, by John Wilhite, Esq.-p. 28

BLANKENSHIP, Jerome & Mary Ann Crain-Nov. 15, 1852, by Waman L. Woods-p. 43

BLANKENSHIP, John & Margaret J. Rochhold-Aug. 13, 1852-p. 42

BLANKENSHIP, John & Margaret J. Price-Sept. 13, 1852-p. 43

BLANKENSHIP, Jonathan & Sarah Hutson-Aug. 9, 1853, by W. L. Woods, Esq.-p. 45

BOGER, Fletcher A. & Nancy White-Jan. 6, 1853, by Rev. J. H. Richey-p. 43

BOHANON, Campbell & Rosa Henry-Nov. 19, 1848, by Rev. Thomas Stone-p. 30

BOHANNON, Crockett & Mary Clark-Mar. 4, 1854, by David Snodgrass, Esq.-p. 47

BOHANNON, James & Elvira Roberson-May 26, 1853, by Wm. C. Johnson-p. 44

BOHANON, James J. & Jane England-Dec. 18, 1845, by David Snodgrass, Esq.-p. 21

BOHANON, Jesse & Hasty Randals-Oct. 20, 1848, by Rev. Wm. Burden-p. 30

BOHANNON, Lewis, Jr. & Sarah Williams-Sept. 5, 1841, by Wm. Hudgens, Esq.-p. 12

BOHANNON, Lewis, Senr. & Catherine Henry-Mar. 6, 1851, by Wm. C. Johnson, Esq.-p.37

BOHANNON, Thos. & Jane Kinnard-Dec. 29, 1839, by Jas. Bartlett, Esq.-p. 7

BOHANNON, Wm. & Mahala Clark-Nov. 7, 1841, by Wm. Hudgens, Esq.-p. 13

BOHANNON, Wm. C. & Elizabeth McCormick-Feb. 4, 1851, by Wm. C. Johnson, Esq.-p.37

BOLIN, Isham & Malinda Davis-Oct. 1, 1852, p. 42

BOLIN, Samuel & Margaret Ann Scarbrough-Mar. 15, 1855, by Wm. M. Anderson, Esq.-p. 50

BORDEN, Samuel & Elizabeth Gamble-May 3, 1846, by M. C. Dibrell, Esq.-p. 23

BOSSON, Wm., Jr. & Jane Cummings-Sept. 27, 1847-p. 26

BOUNDS, Thos. & Mary Isham-Aug. 26, 1844, by Rev. Thos. Stone-p. 18

BOUTON, Wm. & Susan Davis-June 10, 1852, by John Crook, Esq.-p. 41

BOWLIN, George & Mary Gay-Oct. 6, 1843, by Rev. John Yates-p. 16

BOWMAN, Andrew J. & Susan Denton-Sept. 13, 1842, by Thos. Green, Esq.-p. 14

BOWMAN, Bethel & Elender Burgess-Apr. 6, 1840, by Rev. Levi Perkins-p. 8

BOWMAN, Henry E. & Mahaly Thomas-Jan. 3, 1849-p. 31

BOWMAN, Iredell & Polly Ann Gear-July 17, 1851, by Jesse L. Sewell-p. 38

BOWMAN, J. A. & Tempa Johnson-July 31, 1856, by L. H. Bennett, Esq.-p. 53

BOWMAN, Jeremiah & Elizabeth Saunders-May 10, 1854, by John L. Grissom, Esq.-p.48

BOWMAN, Lewis P. & Mary Whitson-Feb. 5, 1840, by Sims Dearing, Esq.-p. 7

BOWMAN, Wm. & Dolly Whitson-July 2, 1839-p. 5

BOYD, Benjamin F. & Louisa Lyda-July 24, 1851, by Rev. G. W. Lentz-p. 38

BOYD, Henry & Charlotte Burden-Dec. 18, 1840, by Anderson S. Rogers, Esq.-p. 10

BOYD, Hiram & Paulina Roberts-Dec. 19, 1850, by Abram Saylors, Esq.-p. 36

BOYD, John L. & Sarah Lyda-Apr. 15, 1852, by Rev. Irvin Jones-p. 41

BOYD, Thomas & Jane Lewis-Oct. 22, 1858, by Wm. Wilson, Esq.-p. 59

BOYD, Wm. H. & Harriett McConnel-Nov. 5, 1846-p. 24

BOZARTH, John & Susan Singleton-Oct. 30, 1847-p. 27

BOZARTH, Samuel C. & Elizabeth Robbins-Oct. 19, 1851, by Rev. R. R. Richey-p.39

BRADFORD, Bennet & Louisa Dickerson-Dec. 17, 1840, by Wm. C. Bounds-p. 10

BRADFORD, Thos. & Rebecca Kin-Aug. 23, 1838, by David Snodgrass-p. 2

BRADFORD, Thos. & Margaret Mason-Nov. 6, 1856, by Rev. Thos. Stone-p. 54

BRADFORD, Wm. & Nancy F. Stewart-Dec. 24, 1857, by Rev. Wm. Jared-p. 57

BRADLEY, Charles H. & Mary Ann Bowman-Oct. 17, 1852, by Wm. C. Johnson, Esq.-p.42

BRADLEY, (?)Jonas O. & Sarah C. Bradley-Feb. 14, 1855, by Richard Bradley, Esq.-p. 50

BRAMLET, Vance & Amanda Patterson-Apr. 23, 1856, by Rev. Wm. Jared-p. 53

BRAY, Henry & Mary Bryan-Sept. 7, 1853, by Rev. Levi Perkins-p. 45

BRAZEAL, Elijah & Nancy D. Andrews-Sept. 26, 1849, by Wm. R. Tucker, Esq.-p.32

BREWER, John J. & Sarah Fields-May 18, 1855-p. 50

BREWINGTON, Joseph & Sarah Adams-Dec. 21, 1848, by John Madewell, Esq.-p. 30

BREWINGTON, Reuben & Linda Adams-Mar. 10, 1850, by John Madewell, Esq.-p. 34

BREWSTER, James H. & Emaline Nolen-Aug. 19, 1851, by Rev. G. W. Lentz-p. 38

BRIANT [BRYAN], John & Eglantine S. Yeager-Aug. 15, 1847, by Solomon Yeager, J.P. p. 26

BRIANT, Jourdan & Elizabeth Allison-Apr. 4, 1852, by Rev. Levi Perkins-p. 41

BRITE, John D. & Tlitnea Boulden-Apr. 25, 1844, by Rev. John Yates-p. 17

BROCK, Sam'l. & Nancy Walling-Sept. 24, 1838, by John Bryan-p. 3

BROGDEN, Wiley B. & Louisa Jane White-July 1, 1854-p. 48

BRONSON, Charles & Catharine Jones-Nov. 30, 1856, by Rev. R. R. Richey-p. 54

BRONSON, Dwight & Almyra Ward-Mar. 3, 1857, by Rev. W. Martin-p. 55

BRONSON, Dwight & Almyra Ward-Apr. 19, 1857, by C. S. Eastland, Esq.-p. 55

BRONSON, Robt. L. & Mrs. Mary A. Lane-Jan. 7, 1858, by Wm. Clayton, Esq.-p. 57

BROWN, Benjamin L. & Arazilla Bohannon-Nov. 2, 1853, by Rev. Thos. Stone-p. 46

BROWN, Chas. & Susanah Parks-July 3, 1844, by Robt. Hitchcock, Esq.-p. 18

BROWN, David & Mrs. Margaret Hill-Aug. 2, 1841, by Rev. Corder Stone-p. 11

BROWN, Gideon & Wincy Suttle-Dec. 18, 1845, by Rev. Thos. Stone-p. 22

BROWN, Hiram & Hester Bartlett-Sept. 8, 1850, by Jesse B. Clark, Esq-p. 35

BROWN, Hugh & Lavinnia McGuire-Nov. 4, 1841, by David Snodgrass, Esq.-p. 12

BROWN, Jackson & Elizabeth Lundy-July 21, 1845, by Richard Bradley, Esq.-p. 19

BROWN, James & Mary Ann Holder-May 25, 1843, by Elijah W. Denton, Esq.-p. 15

BROWN, Jesse W. & Emily E. Miller-Aug. 11, 1852, by Andrew Graham, Esq.-p. 42

BROWN, John & Elleanor Barnes-Aug. 28, 1853, by J. D. Hyder, Esq.-p. 45

BROWN, John A. & Jane Henry [Hensey]-July 20, 1845, by Rev. Jesse E. Hickman-p.19

BROWN, Joseph & Eliza Hammonds-Mar. 7, 1850-p. 34

BROWN, Joseph & Nancy Jones-July 14, 1850, by Wm. Clayton, Esq.-p. 35

BROWN, Joseph & Martha J. Mitchell-May 22, 1851, by Rev. M. Y. Brockett-p. 38

BROWN, Lawson & Amanda Hudgens-Jan. 18, 1855, by Rev. Wm. Jared-p. 49

BROWN, Levi & Lucinda Harden-May 12, 1841, by Rev. James Simmons-p. 11

BROWN, Lindsey & Nancy McPherson-Mar. 12, 1849-p. 31

BROWN, Philip & Lewiza Warner-Feb. 25, 1846, by John Pennington-p. 24

BROWN, Samuel & Rebecca Henry-Sept. 8, 1853, by Rev. Miles W. McConnell-p. 45

BROWN, Thomas & Margaret Weaver-May 26, 1840, by Geo. Defrees, Esq.-p. 8

BROWN, Vance M. & Hannah Dearing-Feb. 18, 1850-p. 34

BROWN, Waman (?)I. & Mary E. Evans-June 17, 1858, by John J. Duncan, Esq.-p. 58

BROWN, Wm. & Sophronia Hickey-July 9, 1855, by David Snodgrass, Esq.-p. 50

BROWN, Wm. H. & Ruth A. Bounds-July 28, 1853, by Rev. Thos. Stone-p. 45

BROYLES, Daniel & Catherine Hennessee-Aug. 4, 1842, by David Snodgrass, Esq.-p.13

BROYLES, Hosea & Elizabeth Sperry-Jan. 1, 1857, by Rev. W. C. Haislip-p. 55

BROYLES, John & [Mrs.] Sarah Wisdom [widow of Wm.]-June 2, 1844, by Solomon Yeager, Esq.-p. 18

BROYLES, John & Lucretia Belcher-Dec. 12, 1854, by Wm. Clayton, Esq.-p. 49

BROYLES, John S. & Mary A. Crook-Jan. 18, 1853, by John Whaley, M.G.-p. 43

BRUMLEE, Vardeman & Nancy Hodges-June 28, 1838, by John Gillentine, Esq.-p. 2

BRUMLEY, Jesse & Susan Grantham-Sept. 8, 1842-p. 14

BRUMLEY, John & Sarah Grantham-June 21, 1838, by John Gillentine, Esq.-p. 2

BRUSTER, Thos. J. & Emily E. Meek-Feb. 23, 1848, by M. C. Dibrell, Esq.-p. 28

BRYAN [See also, BRIANT]
BRYAN, James H. & Nancy J. Greene-Oct. 20, 1857, by Rev. M. Y. Brockett-p. 56
[Is this a double wedding? See: Thos. L. Sperry. She was dau. of Wm. & Mary (Fryer) Green.]

BRYAN, Morgan W. & Ann Jane Herd-July 2, 1838, by John Bryan, Esq.-p. 2

BRYAN, Wm. M., Jr. & Mahala Wallis-Apr. 13, 1843, by Wm. Green, Esq.-p. 15

BUCK, Henderson & Christiana Poteet-July 15, 1839, by Jas. Bartlett, Esq.-p. 6

BUCKNER, Berry & Hannah Whitaker-Mar. 10, 1839, by Isaac Buck, Esq.-p. 5

BUCKNER, John J. & Mary Ann Matlock-Jan. 27, 1851, by Wm. Clayton-p. 36

BULLOCK, Thomas R. & Naoma Brown-Mar. 5, 1840, by Wm. C. Bounds, Esq.-p. 8

BUMBALOUGH, Wm. & Lucinda Broyles-Aug. 30, 1847-p. 26

BURAM, Peter & Nancy Burum-Dec. 11, 1853, by Rev. Jeremiah Webb-p. 46

BURDEN, Henry & Miss Fanny White-Nov. 11, 1845, by Rev. Wm. Burden-p. 21

BURDEN, John & Sally White-Nov. 9, 1843, by Robt. H. McManus-p. 16

BURGESS, Hiram & Nancy G. Campbell-May 24, 1838, by Rev. Levi Perkins-p. 2

BURGESS, John R. & Peggy Phy-Feb. 3, 1852, by Thomas Stone, Elder-p. 40

BURTON, Edmund & Nancy Billings-July 23, 1846, by Rev. Thos. Stone-p. 24

BUSSELL, Geo. L. & Nancy Farley-Sept. 11, 1848, by Abraham Saylors, Esq.-p. 29

BUSSELL, Ingraham & Lucinda Bear-Mar. 3, 1853, by Rev. Wm. Goodwin-p. 44

BUSSELL, John W. & Lucinda Howell-Oct. 12, 1846-p. 24

BUSSELL, Prestley & Elizabeth Howell-Oct. 25, 1839, by Rev. Josiah Williams-p.6

BUSSELL, Rhodom & Amy Brown-Feb. 18, 1846, by John Wilhite, Esq.-p. 22

BUSSELL, Wm. C. T. & Eliza Jane Deweese-Mar. 15, 1843, by Wm. Glenn, Esq.-p. 15

BUSSY, Jamison & Mary Denny-Dec. 2, 1838, by John Gillentine, Esq.-p. 3

BUTHRAM, James & Phebe Kathcart-Oct. 1, 1855-p. 51

BUTRAM, James & Hannah Conly-Jan. 2, 1859, by Richard Bradly, Esq.-p. 59

BUTRAM, John & Mary Ann Beshears-Aug. 7, 1850, by Andrew Graham, Esq.-p. 35

BUXTON, John & Frances Gwinn-Mar. 20, 1820-(L.P.-B.V.)

BUXTON, Stephen A. & Pauline Midget-Feb. 22, 1843-p. 15

BUXTON, Stephen G. & Mary Gibbs-Oct. 2, 1839-p. 6

BYNUM, David W. & Blanchey Rogers-Apr. 6, 1848, by Wm. Clayton, Esq.-p. 28

BYNUM, James & Elizabeth Rogers-Nov. 27, 1842, by Robt. H. McManus, Esq.-p. 14

BYNUM, James M. & Mary Jarvis-Oct. 3, 1841, by James Knowles, Esq.-p. 12

BYNUM, Wm. & Nancy Clark-July 9, 1840, by Wm. Knowles, Esq.-p. 9

CALL, Jacob F. & Martha Jane McCance-Dec. 25, 1856, by Rev. Chas. Graham-p. 55

CALL, Joseph, Jr. & Nancy Caroline Graham-Jan. 5, 1854, by Wm. C. Johnson, Esq.-p. 47

CAMERON, G. W. P. & Elizabeth McGhee-June 26, 1856, by Rev. Jesse E. Hickman-p.53

CAMERON, James M. & Eliza Jones-June 5, 1842, by Thos. Jones, Esq.-p. 13

CAMMORN, Thos. & Sarah Hayse-Mar. 15, 1849, by A. J. Sims, Esq.-p. 31

CAMP, H. J. & Julia Warren-Jan. 9, 1856, by Rev. M. Y. Brockett-p. 52

CAMPBELL, Daniel & Patsy Ellison-Sept. 4, 1811-(L.P.-B.V.)

CAMPBELL, Matthew & Delila Nash-Apr. 10, 1840, by Rev. Levi Perkins-p. 8

CANARD, David & Judith Howard-Aug. 23, 1844, by Rev. Thos. Stone-p. 18

CANTREL, Geo. W. & Nancy Ann Baker-Dec. 3, 1855-p. 52

CANTRELL, Paris & Rose Anna Fryes-July 28, 1853, by Joseph Gist, Esq.-p. 45

CANTRELL, Starling & Mary Crowder-Sept. 3, 1856-p. 54

CARDWELL, Washington & Polly Hitchcock-Nov. 7, 1838-p. 3

CARIG, Wm. & Juliana Spur-Mar. 8, 1846, by David Snodgrass, Esq.-p. 22

CARMICHAEL, John S. & Sarah D. Little-Aug. 9, 1852, by Wm. C. Johnson-p. 42

CARRICK, Hugh L. & Matilda J. Leftwich-Feb. 25, 1841, by Rev. Jesse E. Hickman-p. 10

CARRICK, Isaac L. & Lucy R. Ussery-June 30, 1835-(L.P.-B.V.)

CARRICK, John A. & Mrs. Susan H. Carrick-Aug. 10, 1843, by Wm. R. Tucker, Esq.-p. 16

CARRICK, John M. & Mary Mitchell-May 8, 1851, by Rev. J. E. Hickman-p. 38

CARROLL, Ezekiel & Elizabeth Davis-May 27, 1857, by J. W. Mitchell, Esq.-p. 56

CARROLL, Jesse & Nancy Earles-Nov. 15, 1853, by C. A. Taylor, Esq.-p. 46

CARROLL, Samuel S. & Julia A. Steele-Oct. 5, 1854, by Rev. Wm. Goodman[Goodwin?] p. 49

CARTER, Peter, Jr. & Olevy Dillion-May 2, 1856, by Rev. W. B. Huddleston-p. 53

CARTER, Wm. F. & Priscilla D. Gillentine-Nov. 20, 1838, by Thos. Green, Esq.-p.3

CARTER, Wm. F. & Mary Ann Dunn-May 29, 1847-p. 26

CASH, Elias & Mary Savage-Aug. 9, 1846, by Rev. Thos. Stone-p. 23

CASH, John & Jane Gooch-Mar. 19, 1840, by Rev. Corder Stone-p. 8

CASHDOLLAR, Samuel A. & Sarah E. Glenn-Nov. 8, 1853, by Rev. Miles W. McConnell-p. 46

CASS, Richard & Louisa McConnell-Mar. 3, 1846-p. 22

CATHCART, Daniel & Mary Howard-Mar. 19, 1848, by Rev. A. McBride-p. 28

CAVANESS, Geo. & Sophronia Dew-Jan. 8, 1856, by Alvey Bussell, Esq.-p. 52

CHANDLER, Sam'l. B. & Martha Crowder-Jan. 23, 1840, by C. Sulivent-p. 7

CHARLES, Arlington J. & Martha E. Delafield-Oct. 11, 1840, by Wm. Knowles, Esq.-p. 9

CHARLES, James & Jane Hooten-Oct. 6, 1842-p. 14

CHARLES, James & Eliza Templeton-Feb. 12, 1852-p. 40

CHARLES, Stephen K. & Polly Knowles-Sept. 29, 1817-(L.P.-B.V.)

CHRISTIAN, James H. & Catharine Gear-Aug. 4, 1839, by Sims Dearing, Esq.-p. 5

CHRISTIAN, Moffitt A. & Frances Moore-Feb. 25, 1855, by Rev. M.Y. Brockett-p.50

CLARK, Christopher & Sarah Walling-Dec. 18, 1858, by Jos. W. Clark, Esq.-p. 59

CLARK, Darius & Mary Ann McDaniel-Apr. 21, 1852, by Isaac Denton, M.G.-p. 41

CLARK, Isaac P. & Dicey Henry-Oct. 20, 1853, by Rev. Thos. Stone-p. 46

CLARK, Isaiah & Margaret Harris-Sept. 18, 1853, by Rev. Thos. E. Hutson-p. 46

CLARK, James & Mary Walling-Feb. 28, 1856-p. 53

CLARK, Jesse & Melonia Couch-Jan. 5, 1847-p. 25

CLARK, Joseph, Jr. & Keziah McGowen-Nov. 10, 1844, by Rev. Arnold Moss-p. 18

CLARK, Sam'l. & Paralee Hart-Oct. 19, 1850-p. 35

CLARK, Waman & Elizabeth Lowery-Feb. 28, 1843, by Rev. Jesse E. Hickman-p. 15

CLARK, Wm. & Amerilla Julin-Mar. 6, 1847-p. 25

CLENNY, James T. & Malinda Rowland-Apr. 17, 1839, by Rev. G. W. Martin-p. 5

CLINE, George & Bethia Hunter-Mar. 3, 1847-p. 25

CLOUSE, Benjamin & Susannah Suttle-Sept. 11, 1845, by Rev. Thos. Stone-p. 22

CLOUSE, Francis M. & Elizabeth Bussell-Apr. 30, 1856, by B. Hitchcock, Esq.-p.53

CLOUSE, Wm. H. & Caroline V. Lewis-July 4, 1841, by James Knowles, Esq.-p. 11

CLOUSE, Wm. R. & Lucilla Randolph-Feb. 1, 1854, by J. H. Isom, Esq.-p. 47

CLOYD, James E. & Polly Ann Wilhite-Sept. 22, 1843(?)-by John Wilhite, Esq.-p. 14.[This marriage fell between those for Sept. 18, & Oct. 13, 1842.]

COATNEY, Samuel F. & Clementine H. Henry-Sept. 13, 1855, by Rev. J.E. Hickman-p.51

CODY, Milton H. & Ann Fiske-Apr. 7, 1858, by M. C. Dibrell-p. 57

COLE, Christopher C. & Sarah A. Saylors-May 2, 1850-p. 34

COLE, James & Susan Doyle-Aug. 29, 1854, by Elijah W. Denton, Esq.-p. 49

COLE, John & Catharine Rhea-Sept. 11, 1849, by W. W. Moore, Esq.-p. 32

COLE, Josiah J. & Mary Grasty-Dec. 27, 1849, by Rev. John Yates-p. 33

COLE, Wm. & Martha Ramsey-Jan. 7, 1840, by Rev. John H[enry] Mann-p. 7

COLE, Wm. R. & Jane Parks-Sept. 23, 1844, by Alvey Bussell, Esq.-p. 18

COLEMAN, Amhurst & Tennessee Usrey-Jan. 14, 1858, by Wm. Clayton, Esq.-p. 57

COLLIER, James & Susannah Atkinson-Nov. 21, 1839, by Asa Certain, Esq.-p. 6

COLVIN [CALVIN?], Micajah & Nancy Baker-Oct. 22, 1846-p. 24

COMPTON, Geo. & Mary Snodgrass-Jan. 8, 1852, by Rev. J. E. Hickman-p. 40

COMPTON, John P. & Mary F. Vass-Dec. 6, 1849, by Rev. Wm. Jared-p. 33

CONNER, James R. & Cynthia B. Mennifee-Dec. 22, 1842, by Anderson S. Rogers, Esq.-p. 14

CONWAY, Lewis P. & Margaret E. Grime-Jan. 25, 1854, by Rev. Nathan Judd-p. 47

COOK, Absolum & Jane Willson-Mar. 25, 1841, by James Knowles, Esq.-p. 11

COOK, Earl J. & Eliza Cunningham-Mar. 19, 1840, by John Gillentine, Esq.-p. 8

COOK, James & Evaline Matlock-Mar. 11, 1851, by Rev. J. B. Wynns-p. 37

COOK, John & Polly Rickman-July 30, 1835-(L.P.-B.V.)

COOKE, Wm. M. & Talitha A. Dearing-Jan. 27, 1859, by M. C. Dibrell, Esq.-p. 59

COOPER, Eli & Elinda Adcock-Dec. 24, 1846-p. 25

COOPER, Nathan & Sally Montgomery-Oct. 13, 1846-p. 24

COOPER, Samuel & Sarah Ann Patton-Dec. 14, 1847-p. 27

COOPER, Welcome P. & Eliza Tucker-Oct. 21, 1841, by R. H. McManus-p. 12

COPE, Andrew J. & Lucinda Keathly-Jan. 1, 1846, by Rev. D. Coulson-p. 21

COPE, James M. & Sarah Ann McGarr-Feb. 20, 1856, by Rev. L. H. Bennett-p. 52

COPE, Jesse & Jane Milam-Dec. 18, 1856, by L. H. Bennett, M.G.-p. 54

COPE, Joshua M. & Pernetta C. Keathly-Dec. 4, 1856, by Rev. Wm. Jared-p. 54

COPE, John W. & Sarah Sims-Nov. 22, 1838, by Jesse Walling, Esq.-p. 3

COPE, Madison & Sarah C. White-Oct. 31, 1855-p. 51

COPE, Madison K. & Elizabeth Meek-Jan. 18, 1844, by Wm. Austin, Esq.-p. 17

COPE, Marshall & Elizabeth McGarr-Nov. 25, 1858, by Rev. L. H. Bennett-p. 59

COPE, Mason L. & Amanda C. Keathley-June 30, 1853, by Rev. Thos. E. Hutson-p.45

COPE, Stephen D. & Elizabeth Green-Jan. 17, 1843, by Rev. Ozias Denton-p. 14
[She was grd-dau. of Rev. John Green; dau. of Thos. & Delilah (Stype).]

COPE, Wallace B. & Clarissa J. Sims-Sept. 3, 1846, by Rev. J. Herd-p. 23

COPE, Wiley & Helen Cantrell-July 15, 1858, by J. L. Grissom, Esq.-p. 58

COPE, Wm. A. & Nancy Cope-Aug. 2, 1849, by Rev. James Herd-p. 32

COPELAND, _____ W. & Margaret Beaty-Feb. 6, 1839-p. 4

COPELAND, Robt. & Margarett Dunn-Aug. 19, 1858, by Rev. Elisha Webb-p. 58

COPELAND, Wm. & Sarah Gist-Jan. 8, 1856-p. 52

COPELAND, Wm. E. & Nancy Jane Walker-Oct. 30, 1851, by David Snodgrass-p. 39

CORDER, Jesse & Nancy Mitchell-Mar. 14, 1849-p. 31

CORDER, Wm. & Julia Ann Sweat-July 30, 1854, by Rich. Bradley, Esq.-p. 48

CORNELIOUS, James T. & Phebe Ann Walling-Jan. 17, 1855, by Rev. Wm. Jared-p. 49

COSBY, Williamson & Delina S. Scott-Apr. 23, 1846, by Jesse Hickman-p. 22

COTTEN, Reuben C. & Eleanor W. Hutson-May 27, 1848, by Rev. T. E. Hutson-p. 28

COTTEN, Wm. F. & Patience Landrum-Mar. 13, 1839-p. 4

COUCH, Timothy & Jane Pennington-Feb. 1, 1842, by Rev. Ozias Denton-p. 13

COURTNEY, Landon & Frances Bright-Aug. 6, 1857, by Z. Hitchcock, Esq.-p. 56

COX, Robt. & Mrs. Mary Armstrong-Oct. 24, 1836-(L.P.-B.V.)

COYLE, Enoch & Ruth Berry-NO DATE, but between Aug. 16 & 29, 1839-p. 5

COZART, Wm. N. & Sarah Odle [Odell?]-Feb. 16, 1842, by Jas. Knowles, Esq.-p. 13

CRAFORD, Harvey S. & Lydia F. McVilanie-Sept. 24, 1848, by Rev. Wm. Jared-p. 29

CRAFT, John & Amanda E. Finney-Nov. 13, 1856, by Wm. Clayton, Esq.-p. 54

CRAIN, Andrew & Mary Badger-July 4, 1852, by Rev. T. E. Hutson-p. 41

CRAIN, James D. & Martha Knowles-Oct. 30, 1856, by Rev. Thos. E. Hutson-p. 54

CRAIN, Wm. & Permelia A. Moore-May 9, 1852, by E. W. Denton, Esq.-p. 41

CRANE, Martin P. & Rachel Mitchell-Mar. 22, 1840, by John Gillentine, Esq.-p. 8

CRAVEN, Bird H. & Julia Ann Olly Latitia Holman-Jan. 29, 1854, by David Snodgrass,
        Esq.-p. 47                    -14-

CRAWFORD, Robt. N. & Lucinda Arnold-Apr. 22, 1841, by Wm. Little, Esq.-p. 11

CRAWLEY, James A. & Nancy Phillips-Oct. 5, 1848, by Rev. Levi Perkins-p. 29

CREWS, James & Nancy Pettit-Oct. 11, 1848, by Rev. M. N. Brockett-p. 30

CROOK, Chas. & Rachel Elvira Wycoff-Feb. 5, 1854, by Isaac Lollar, Esq.-p. 47

CROOK, John, Jr. & Nancy Caroline Barnes-Feb. 10, 1851-p. 37

CROWDER, Henry J. P. & Elizabeth Gardner-Dec. 31, 1849-p. 33

CUMBY, _____ & Jane Grantham-Apr. 1, 1839, by Tilman Brown, Esq.-p. 4

CUMMINGS, James & Elizabeth Meek-Aug. 20, 1848, by Rev. Thos. E. Hutson-p. 29

CUNNINGHAM, James & Virginia Cocks-July 28, 1852, by Jo. G. Mitchell, Esq.-p. 41

CUNNINGHAM, John & Martha Greenfield-Oct. 26, 1850-p. 36

CUNNINGHAM, John & Mary Frasure-Oct. 9, 1854-p. 49

CUTLER, Albigence W. & Rachael Emeline Green-Aug. 10, 1852, by B.M. Stevens-p.42

DALE, Wm. Leonard & Amanda Haston-Mar. 14, 1858, by Wm. Wilson, Esq.-p. 57

DALLEY, Owen & Susan Roberts-Nov. 1, 1846-p. 24

DANIEL, Charles & Brunetta Bohannon-Feb. 6, 1851, by Rev. Thos. Stone-p. 37

DANLEY, Geo. & Jane Grag [Gregg?]-Nov. 28, 1845, by Shadrick Price-p. 22

DAVIS, Almon L. & Louisa Taylor-May 29, 1838, by Rev. J. E. Hickman-p. 2

DAVIS, Arthur & Mary Ann Allen-July 21, 1851, by Jno. L. Grissom, Esq.-p. 38

DAVIS, Calloway & Matilda Flynn-Feb. 17, 1839, by Elijah Frost, Esq.-p. 5

DAVIS, Christopher P. & Pernetta Smith-July 28, 1853, by Rev. J.H. Richey-p. 45

DAVIS, Cornelius & Matilda Tucker-Apr. 8, 1839, by Anderson S. Rogers-p. 5

DAVIS, Ephriam & Sally Clark-July 25, 1838, by Rev. Abel Hutson; Isaac Clark
[Surety?]-p. 2

DAVIS, Geo. & Mary M. Rogers-Feb. 8, 1854, by David Snodgrass, Esq.-p. 47

DAVIS, Henry & Mary Keithley-Sept. 9, 1841, by Rev. James H. Morgan-p. 12

DAVIS, Henry L. & Elizabeth Laskins-Apr. 13, 1852, by Wm. Goodwin-p. 41

DAVIS, Isaac & Nigary Ann Waddle-Oct. 10, 1850, by Wm. Clayton, Esq.-p. 35

DAVIS, James & Louisa Brown-July 26, 1855, by John W. Mitchell, Esq.-p. 51

DAVIS, Jesse & Catharine Potts-Nov. 16, 1845, by Robt. Hitchcock, Esq.-p. 21

DAVIS, John A. & Sarah Swindle-July 27, 1853, by Rev. Thos. E. Hutson-p. 45

DAVIS, John W. & Lucy Ann Kirke-Aug. 26, 1847-p. 26

DAVIS, John W. & Mary Jane Jones-Feb. 4, 1852, by Wm. I. Russell, Esq.-p. 40

DAVIS, Joseph & Edey Dukes-Sept. 29, 1846, by Jos. G. Mitchell-p. 23

DAVIS, Joseph W. & Ellen Gill-Jan. 19, 1843, by Rev. Jesse Cole-p. 14

DAVIS, Maxville & Mary Tacket-Sept. 28, 1838, by Richard Crowder-p. 3

DAVIS, Oliver & Hannah G. Witt-May 29, 1853, by W. L. Woods-p. 44

DAVIS, Robt. & Nancy Womick-Jan. 25, 1849, by J. L. Grisham, Esq.-p. 31

DAVIS, Robert & Susan M. Scarborough-June 25, 1857, by Chas. S. Eastland, Esq.-p. 56

DAVIS, Washy & Polly Jane Good-Dec. 15, 1855, by Rev. Isaac Denton-p. 52

DAVIS, Wiley & Caroline Gentry-Feb. 7, 1851, by Wm. R. Tucker, Esq.-p. 37

DAVIS, Wm. A. & Martha Ann Mitchell-June 8, 1848, by Rev. Levi Perkins-p. 28

DAVIS, Wm. P. & Margaret Jones-Aug. 31, 1851, by T. E. Hutson-p. 38

DEAN, Heron S. & Minerva J. Scott-Aug. 31, 1855, by Wm. Clayton, Esq.-p. 51

DEARING, Abraham B. & Rebecca Robinson-Sept. 11, 1850, by David Snodgrass, Esq.-p. 35

DEARING, Balur [Balus] E. & Nancy Broyles-Aug. 12, 1841, by Rev. J.E. Hickman-p.11

DEARING, John W. & Louisa Dyer-Oct. 11, 1849, by Rev. Thomas Stone-p. 32

DEARING, Quin M. & Telitha Wisdom-June 14, 1842, by Solomaon Yeager, J.P.-p. 13

DEARING, Wm. W. & Ann Johnson Pass-Nov. 25, 1841, by David Snodgrass-p. 12

DEITZ [See: DISTZ]

DEMPSEY, David & Peggy Kyle-Mar. 26, 1834-(L.P.-B.V.)

DENTON, Elijah, Senr. & Mary Sparkman-Oct. 23, 1843, by Rev. James H. Morgan-p.16

DENTON, James R. & Amanda Sparkman-Sept. 21, 1851, by W. L. Woods, Esq.-p. 39

DENTON, Jas. W. & Elizabeth Pennington-Jan. 2, 1840, by Jesse Walling-p. 7

DENTON, Levi B. & Martha Slatten-Oct. 27, 1842, by Elijah W. Denton, Esq.-p. 14

DENTON, Sterling & Judea Province-Jan. 12, 1841-p. 10

DEVLIN, Francis & Martha Benton-Dec. 9, 1846, by Joel Whitley, Esq.-p. 24

DEW, John M. & Lethy Ann Byers-Dec. 22, 1850, by Robt. Hitchcock, Esq.-p. 36

DEW, Sam'l. H. & Matilda K. Hawkins-July 18, 1850, by Rev. Wm. Jared-p. 35

DEWEESE, Meradith & Matilda J. Certain-Feb. 4, 1841, by Rev. S. G. Buxton-p. 10

DIBRELL, Charles C. & Mary E. Jenkins-Dec. 20, 1838, by Rev. G. W. Martin-p. 4

DIBRELL, George G. & Mary E. Leftwich-Jan. 13, 1842, by Rev. S.S. Yarbrough-p.12

DIBRELL, Montgomery C. & Mary Ann E. Eastland-Sept. 1, 1842, by Rev. S. S. Yarbrough-p. 14

DILDINE, Ammon & Mary Hutchins-Dec. 4, 1841, by Thos. Jones, Esq.-p. 12

DILDINE, Hezikiah & Nancy Farley-Dec. 8, 1841, by Asa Certain, Esq.-p. 12

DILDINE, Jonathan & Polly Carey-Nov. 8, 1838, by Richard Crowder-p. 3

DILLION, Clinton & Elizabeth Holder-June 6, 1855, by E. W. Denton, Esq.-p. 50

DILLION, James & Sophah Morris-June 26, 1847-p. 26

DINGES, Wm. & Amanda Fancher-Apr. 29, 1851, by Wm. Clayton, Esq.-p. 38

DINGES, Wm. M. & Emeline Cameron-Sept. 7, 1848, by Rev. Thos. E. Hutson-p. 29

DIRE, Jose C. & Lorinda Byers-June 12, 1846, by Robt. Hitchcock-p. 23

DISTZ [DEITZ], Jonas A. & Frances Street-Mar. 2, 1840-p. 8

DITTY, Francis F. & Allisinia Dyer-Nov. 18, 1846-p. 24

DOBBS, Wm. & Mary Duncan-Nov. 29, 1849-p. 33

DODSON, James & Mary Dodson-Oct. 11, 1855, by John W. Mitchell, Esq.-p. 51

DODSON, Jesse & Mary Caroline Earles-Mar. 22, 1855, by John W. Mitchell, Esq.-
p. 50. [He was son of Solomon.]

DODSON, Jesse, Jr. & Susan Prater-Aug. 15, 1850, by Rev. Zach Anderson-p. 35

DODSON, John & Juda Frazier-Nov. 8, 1838, by John Gillentine-p. 3

DODSON, John H. & Jane Baker-Sept. 6, 1851, by Rev. John Green-p. 39

DODSON, Noah, Jr. & Virginia Hale-Mar. 4, 1855, by John W. Mitchell, Esq.-p. 50

DODSON, Reuben & Rebecca Thompson-June 13, 1839, by Asa Certain-p. 5

DODSON, Samuel & Sarah Ann Earles-Jan. 7, 1855, by John W. Mitchell, Esq.-p. 49

DODSON, Samuel & Amanda Prater-Aug. 30, 1856, by David Snodgrass-p. 54. [He was son of Jesse.]

DODSON, Simpson & Elizabeth Prator-Sept. 28, 1852, by Rev. Zach. Anderson-p. 42

DODSON, Solomon & Elizabeth Wilson-Jan. 15, 1842, by Anderson S. Rogers, Esq.- p. 13

DODSON, Valentine & Julian Dale-Feb. 13, 1840, by Anderson S. Rogers-p. 7. [She was dau. of John, a Revolutionary soldier.]

DONALDSON, Jacob & Mary Ann Pearson-Apr. 15, 1855, by Rev. Wm. Jared-p. 50

DONALDSON, Jacob A. & Nancy E. Brooks-NO DATE. Returned, but not executed, p. 38

DONALDSON, Jacob A. & Catharine S. Call-Jan. 22, 1853, by Rev. Wm. Burden-p. 43

DONNEGAN, Alfred & Susan Dunn-Jan. 26, 1853, by Rev. Levi Perkins-p. 43

DOTSON, Daniel & Emeline Denton-Sept. 15, 1853, by Rev. James Herd-p. 46

DOTSON, John & Sarah Yates-Dec. 2, 1845, by Joseph G. Mitchell, Esq.-p. 21

DOWNEY, James C. & Cynthia J. Stacey-Dec. 11, 1855, by Rev. M. Y. Brockett-p. 52

DOWNEY, Robt. P. D. & Lavina W. Gooch-Aug. 6, 1848, by Rev. W. H. Hooker-p. 29

DOWNING, Robt. J. & Margaret Anderson-Nov. 27, 1838, by Rev. J. H. Morgan-p. 3

DOYLE, Daniel M. & Jane Smith-Sept. 14, 1853, by Rev. Jas. H. Morgan-p. 45

DOYLE, Dawns B. & Emaline Austin-Jan. 31, 1844-p. 17

DOYLE, Simon W. & Jane Gillentine-May 19, 1841, by Rev. John H[enry] Mann-p. 11

DOYLE, Simon W. & Martha Lewis-Mar. 21, 1852, by W. W. Moore, Esq.-p. 41

DOYLE, Wm. & Alzira Wallis-Feb. 9, 1839-p. 4

DRAKE, Charles & Malinda Adkins-Feb. 3, 1840, by Wm. Little, Esq.-p. 7

DRIVER, Burrell & Elizabeth Gay-Nov. 15, 1849, by Rev. Wm. Martin-p. 32

DUGGAN, John W. & Mary Richt-Dec. 7, 1848, by J. D. Hyder, Esq.-p. 30

DUGGER, David A. & Rachel Pollard-June 10, 1853-p. 45

DUGGER, John & Catharine Malinda Bean-Dec. 8, 1853, by John Madewell, Esq.-p.46

DULANEY, J. H. & Sarah Green-Jan. 24, 1859, by Rev. J. H. Stone-p. 59

DULANEY, Sam'l. P. & Hester C. Bronson-Mar. 18, 1855, by Rev. M. Y. Brockett-p.50

DUNAGIN, Wm. & Mary Parks-Mar. 1, 1852-p. 40

DUNCAN, Calloway & Mary Howard-Oct. 9, 1851, by David Snodgrass-p. 39

DUNCAN, James W. & Frances Maria Blankenship-Dec. 18, 1852-p. 43

DUNCAN, John & Susannah Hooper-Aug. 26, 1839-p. 6

DUNCAN, John J. & Susan Austin-Nov. 1, 1855, by Rev. Wm. Jared-p. 51

DUNCAN, John T. & Martha C. Albert-Aug. 29, 1852, by Jas. B. Lowrey, Esq.-p. 42

DUNGY, John & Mary Jane Rickman-Apr. 19, 1842, by Rev. Ozias Denton-p. 13

DUNHAM, Thos. W. & Adaline Mitchell-Mar. 10, 1852, by Wm. Jared-p. 40

DUNN, Geo. A. & Mary Hitchcock-Nov. 3, 1854, by Rev. Levi Perkins-p. 49

DUNN, John Wesley & Mary Bersheba Stewart-June 13, 1858, by M.C. Dibrell, Esq.-p.58

DUNN, John Worley [Washy] & Cornelia Ricks-Aug. 7, 1855, by Wm. Clayton, Esq.-p.51

DUNN, Peter & Elizabeth Henry-June 20, 1838-p. 2

DUNN, Wm. & Martha Ann Ricks-Mar. 15, 1853, by Wm. Clayton, Esq.-p. 44

DUNN, Wm. L. & Hulda R. Rogers-July 25, 1854, by Joab W. Muershon, Esq.-p. 48

DURHAM, George & Mary Jane Poe-Mar. 7, 1848, by John Wilhite, Esq.-p. 28

DUROSSETT, Byron & Malinda McCain-Sept. 4, 1851, by W. R. Tucker, Esq.-p. 38

DUROSSETT, Elias & Lavina R. Lee-Sept. 19, 1855, by R. Simpson, Esq.-p. 51

DUROSSITT, Wm. C. & Kitty Butram-June 28, 1853, by Wm. C. Johnson-p. 45

DYER, David & Margarett Findley-Mar. 8, 1851, by John Crook, Esq.-p. 37

DYER, Nelson & Silah Issom-July 9, 1845, by Rev. B. F. Farrell-p. 19

EARLES, Hosea & Sarah Earles-Jan. 10, 1852-p. 40

EARLES, Joseph & Mary Ann Tindle-Sept. 16, 1857, by Rev. T. L. Denton-p. 56

EARLES, Martin H. & Susan Fox-Jan. 11, 1844, by Robt. H. McManus, Esq.-p. 17

EARLES, Pleasant & Elizabeth W. Baker-Jan. 23, 1840, by Thos. Green, Esq.-p. 7

EARLES, Richmond & Mahala Anderson-Feb. 1, 1856, by Rev. Tidence L. Denton-p.52

EARLES, Wm. & Sarah Owing-Apr. 14, 1844, by John Swindle, Esq.-p. 17

EARLES, Wm. M. & Tabitha Holder-Oct. 17, 1846, by Joel Whitley, Esq.-p. 24

EASTLAND, Chas. S. & Sarah E. Broyles-Oct. 16, 1855, by M.C. Dibrell, Esq.-p.51

EASTLAND, Geo. & Elizabeth Driver-July 29, 1855, by John C. Stevens, Esq.-p. 51

EASTLAND, Robt. M. & Eliza Brazeale-Sept. 12, 1843, by Rev. Jesse Cole-p. 16

EATON, James T. & Malvina Williams-Dec. 18, 1855, by Wm. Clayton, Esq.-p. 52

EDENS, Leonard & Sally Rigsby-July 2, 1828[38?], by Jesse Walling, Esq.-p. 2

ELDER, Anthony H. & Judith Ann Hickman-Mar. 19, 1856, by Rev. M.Y. Brockett-p.53

ELDRIDGE, John D. & Elizabeth Taylor-July 14, 1858, by Alvy Bussell, Esq.-p. 58

ELKINS, John & Mary Hutchins-Jan. 24, 1843, by Thos. Jones, Esq.-p. 14

ELKINS, John G. & Ann Hutchins-Feb. 5, 1843, by Jesse M. Sullivan, Esq.-p. 15
[Is this a double wedding? See: Chas. Hutchings.]

ELLER, Hiram & Matilda Jane Weaver-Apr. 25, 1857-p. 55

ELLIOTT, A. C. & Elizabeth Warner-Jan. 4, 1852, by Rev. Thos. Stone-p. 40

ELLIOTT, Wm. C. & Hulda Howard-Oct. 22, 1857, by D. M. Southard, Esq.-p. 56

ELLIS, Albert L. & Sarah Jane Brown-Apr. 7, 1839(?), by John Pennington, Esq.-p. 11. [Between marriages occurring between June 10 & 14, 1841.]

ELMORE, Geo. W. & Mary C. Brown-Feb. 26, 1851, by Abram Saylors, Esq.-p. 37

ELMORE, Thos. & Elender Matthews-Oct. 17, 1849, by Robt. Hitchcock, Esq.-p. 32

ELMORE, Wm. C. & Evaline Baker-Feb. 2, 1854, by John Crook, Esq.-p. 47

ELMS, Jonathan, Jr. & Matilda Hill-Feb. 9, 1850-p. 34

ELMS, Jones & Elizabeth Evaline Roberson-Jan. 16, 1851, by Wm. C. Johnson, Esq.-p. 36

ELROD, Giles & Senith Howell-Mar. 4, 1847-p. 25

ELROD, Thos. & Elizabeth Nolen-May 7, 1851, by Abram Saylors, Esq.-p. 38

ENGLAND, Aaron G. & Omey Weaver-July 5, 1853, by Wm. C. Johnson-p. 45

ENGLAND, Aaron W. & Mary Walker-Dec. 2, 1850, by Abram Saylors, Esq.-p. 36

ENGLAND, Clabourn & Martha Weatherford-Apr. 19, 1848, by W.K. Bradford, Esq.-p.28

ENGLAND, Crocket & Saraphina C. Hickey-Feb. 17, 1853, by Sam. Usrey, Esq.-p. 44

ENGLAND, Elijah & Jane Weatherford-Dec. 3, 1849-p. 33

ENGLAND, James S. & Milda J. Bowman-Oct. 6, 1848, by Wm. C. Johnson-p. 29

ENGLAND, Matthew & Margaret Anderson-Sept. 3, 1853, by John Crook, Esq.-p. 45

ENGLAND, Robt. & Jane Tittleton-Aug. 3, 1854, by John Willhite, Esq.-p. 48

ENGLAND, Wesley & Aneliza Little-Nov. 2, 1848, by F. S. Little, Esq.-p. 30

EVANS, Abner & Susannah McBride-July 22, 1846, by James Knowles, Esq.-p. 23

EVANS, Andrew J. & Malviny Corbit-Aug. 30, 1849, by Wm. Clayton, Esq.-p. 32

EVANS, McLen & Mary Wallis-Sept. 21, 1847-p. 26

EVANS, Richard & Catherine Davis-Apr. 18, 1847-p. 25

EVANS, Wm. C. & Margaret Payne-Jan. 15, 1852, by Wm. Clayton, Esq.-p. 40

EVANS, Wm. R. & Mary E. McManus-Jan. 7, 1852, by Wm. Clayton, Esq.-p. 40

FANCHER, Thomas H. & Susannah Officer-Feb. 16, 1840, p. 7

FANCHER, Thos. H. & Eliza Bryan-Feb. 16, 1854, by Rev. M. Y. Brockett-p. 47

FARLEY, David & Elizabeth Willhite-Aug. 1, 1852, by Rev. Thos. Stone-p. 42

FARLEY, Edward & Janetta Wilhite-Jan. 31, 1855, by Henry J. Lyda, Esq.-p. 50

FARLEY, Edward & Martha Jane Clouse-Oct. 1, 1856, by Alvey Bussell, Esq.-p. 54

FARLEY, George & Mary Cooper-Jan. 16, 1849, by A. J. Sims, Esq.-p. 30

FARLEY, Houston & Elizabeth M. Howard-Aug. 13, 1857, by Jas. H. Isom, Esq.-p.56

FARLEY, (?)Joel & Caroline Broyles-Dec. 15, 1850, by Rev. J. L. Sewell-p. 36

FARLEY, John & Izabella A. Albright-Mar. 4, 1847-p. 25

FARLEY, Nathaniel & Martha A. Taylor-Jan. 31, 1857-p. 55

FARLEY, Simpson & Elizabeth Isom-Apr. 1, 1841, by John Pennington, Esq.-p. 11

FARLEY, Solomon & Jane Broyles-Aug. 11, 1844, by Solomon Yeager, Esq.-p. 18

FARLEY, Stephen & Nancy Cash-Jan. 17, 1856, by James H. Irvin, Esq.-p. 52

FARLEY, Stephen & Elizabeth Rice-Dec. 4, 1856, by Alvey Bussell, Esq.-p. 54

FARMER, Jerimiah W. & Miss Adaline Cook-Mar. 13, 1845-p. 19

FARRELL, Andrew & Elizabeth Williams-Nov. 8, 1847, by John Wilhite, Esq.-p. 27

FARRISS, John & Mary Jane Whitson-Apr. 21, 1850, by Shade Price, Esq.-p. 34

FELTON, Joseph B. & Drusilla Mitchell-July 16, 1840, by Thomas Green, Esq.-p. 9

FERGUSON, Alexander & Amanda Mason-Aug. 12, 1849, by John L. Grissom Esq.-p. 32

FERRELL, Archy & Mary Haly-Nov. 3, 1848, by F. S. Little-p. 30

FIN, John & Deniza Pettit-Jan. 11, 1853, by E. W. Denton, Esq.-p. 43

FINLEY, Absolom & Eliza Taylor-Feb. 21, 1848-p. 28

FINLEY, Hugh & Temperence Self-Sept. 30, 1855, by Wm. M. Anderson, Esq.-p. 51

FINDLY, Hugh & Caroline Brown-Nov. 16, 1850-p. 36

FINNIE, James W. & Lucretia Payne-Oct. 5, 1856, by Rev. J. H. Richey-p. 54

FISHER, Alfred & Sarah Hutson-June 19, 1852, by Rev. A. G. Copeland-p. 41

FISHER, Ambrose & Cynthia Clark-Dec. 13, 1851-p. 39

FISHER, Geo. W. & Julia Ann Hutson-Dec. 23, 1855, by Rev. Isaac C. Woodward-p.52

FISHER, James & Susan Hutson-Aug. 2, 1839, by Rev. Abel Hutson-p. 5

FISHER, John P. & Margaret Wright-Oct. 13, 1858, by Rev. T. E. Hutson-p. 58

FISKE, Milton & Helen Scott-Sept. 17, 1857, by J. J. Duncan, Esq.-p. 56

FISKE, Ormel & Lucinda S. F. Denton-Mar. 9, 1843, by Rev. S. S. Yarbrough-p. 15

FLINN, John W. & Malinda J. Hale-June 16, 1854, by J. C. Stevens, Esq.-p. 48

FLINN, Wm. & Elizabeth C. Hencley-Nov. 6, 1846-p. 24

FLOYD, Anderson & Elizabeth Jane Roberts-Feb. 4, 1853, by Rev. J. J. James-p.44

FLOYD, John W. & Eliza J. Snodgrass-Oct. 10, 1854, by Rev. M. Y. Brockett-p. 49

FLOYD, Joseph & Tempy L. M. Ledbetter-May 7, 1857-p. 55

FLYNN, Benjamin & Sally Mooneyham-Jan. 6, 1842, by Rev. John Yates-p. 12

FORD, John E. & Mary Ana Graham-Apr. 18, 1854, by Rev. Wm. Burden-p. 48

FOSTER, Dennis & Dorcas Barnes-Jan. 24, 1841, by Anderson S. Rogers, Esq.-p. 10

FOSTER, Preston & Manerva Lewis-Feb. 21, 1853-p. 44

FOX, John & Elizabeth Bohannon-Oct. 5, 1837-(L.P.-B.V.)

FOX, Joshua & Susan Jane Rutledge-May 30, 1847-p. 26

FOX, Wm. & Malinda Holman-May 29, 1838, by David Snodgrass, Esq.-p. 2

FOX, Wm. & Mahaly J. Kerby-June 29, 1850-p. 35

FRAME, Francis M. & Wildy Hambrick-Dec. 7, 1858, by Richard Bradly, Esq.-p. 59

FRANKLIN, Jeremiah R. & Mary Colly-Sept. 13, 1838, by Wm. Bruster, Esq.-p. 3

FRANKS, Henry & Dysey Witt-Mar. 9, 1851, by Elijah W. Denton, Esq.-p. 37

FRANKS, John W. & Martha Holder-Oct. 26, 1847-p. 27

FRANKS, Wm. & Eliza Holder-Apr. 29, 1851-p. 38

FRASURE, Asa & Eliza Dodson-Nov. 14, 1854, by Rev. Zachariah Anderson-p. 49

FRASURE, Geo. & Sarah Hembrick-June 1, 1854, by O. H. P. Sims, Esq.-p. 48

FRASURE, John & Nancy Miller-Feb. 16, 1840, by Anderson Rogers-p. 7

FRASURE, Ransom & Agness Stewart-July 12, 1853, by Wm. C. Johnson-p. 45

FRAZIER, Henry & Jemima Miller-July 24, 1838-p. 2

FRAZIER, Thos. & Mary Tucker-Nov. 25, 1838, by John Gillentine, Esq.-p. 3

FRAZURE, Richmond & Susannah Dodson-Apr. 23, 1840, by Anderson S. Rogers, Esq.-p. 8

FRAZURE, Wm. & Elizabeth Dunaway-Apr. 25, 1840, by Anderson S. Rogers, Esq.-p.8

FRAZURE, Wm. C. & Nancy Welch-Feb. 2, 1840, by Anderson S. Rogers, Esq.-p. 7

FREEMAN, Doctor S. & Sally Smith-Nov. 5, 1839, by Rev. Arnold Moss-p. 6

FREEMAN, Wm. H. & Nancy Brock-July 20, 1839-p. 5

FRENCH, James H. & Elvira Rice-July 10, 1844, by Rev. A. M. Stone-p. 18

FRISBY, James & Mary Howard-July 7, 1839, by Asa Certain-p. 5

FROST, Joseph & Eliza J. Anderson-Feb. 5, 1848-p. 27

FROST, Matthew & Margaret C. Robinson-Mar. 17, 1854, by John Crook, Esq.-p. 47

FURGASON, Hubbard S. & Nancy Moss-June 24, 1847-p. 26

GAMBLE, Chas. R. & Emily F. Cameron-Oct. 9, 1851, by Rev. Rich. Simpson-p. 39

GAMBLE, John & Mary Foster-Aug. 31, 1856, by Wm. Wilson, Esq.-p. 54

GARDENER, Jackson & Easther J. Edington-Mar. 27, 1847-p. 25

GARROTT, Uriah D. & Letitia Whitley-Apr. 26, 1848, by Wm. Clayton, Esq.-p. 28

GASKEY, John & Adline (?)Roslir-May 19, 1846, by Wm. Glenn, Esq.-p. 23

GATES, John & Mary Netherton-Apr. 7, 1854, by O. H. P. Sims, Esq.-p. 48

GEAR, Wm. J. & Martha Gear-Feb. 5, 1848, by Thos. Cooper, Esq.-p. 27

GEER, Robt. W. & Jane Savage-June 10, 1852, by Rev. M. W. McConnell-p. 41

GENTRY, Henry W. & Luncinda Tucker-Nov. 18, 1857, by Rev. Joseph B. Wynns-p. 56

GENTRY, John W. & Mary L. Whittley-July 5, 1853, by Rev. Wm. Burden-p. 45

GENTRY, Owing & Leann Williams-Dec. 4, 1856, by Wm. Clayton, Esq.-p. 54

GHASKY, Wm. & Elizabeth Webster-Jan. 30, 1846, by M. C. Dibrell, Esq.-p. 22

GIBBONS, Matthew S. & Sarah A. Sperry-Dec. 24, 1851, by M. Y. Brockett-p. 40

GIBBS, Barter & Mary Marcum-Nov. 19, 1840, by Wm. Knowles, Esq.-p. 9

GIBBS, Barton & Priscilla Odle [Odell?]-Apr. 27, 1840-p. 8

GILL, Samuel & Malinda Davis-July 12, 1838, by Joshua Mason, Esq.-p. 2

GILL, Thomas & Malinda Rodgers-Dec. 17, 1857, by M. C. Dibrell, Esq.-p. 57

GILLENTINE, David & Louisa Holderfield-Sept. 16, 1847-p. 26

GILLENTINE, John W. & Minerva Bryan-Oct. 4, 1847-p. 26

GILLENTINE, Robt. G. & Mary Emily Little-Jan. 30, 1853, by Levi Jarvis, Esq.-p.43

GILLENTINE, Wm. L. & Sarah Jett-Feb. 18, 1851, by Rev. Wm. Jared-p. 37

GIST, Benjamin & Martha Ann Webb-Nov. 29, 1849, by C. A. Taylor, Esq.-p. 33

GIST, John & Susan Jane Green-July 11, 1854, by Rev. James Herd-p. 48

GIST, Joseph & Phebe Walling-Sept. 10, 1840, by Thos. Green, Esq.-p. 9

GIST, Joseph & Margaret Anderson-Mar. 23, 1843, by Wm. Green, Esq.-p. 15

GIST, Julias & Ruth Walling-Mar. 29, 1846, by Rev. Isaac Denton-p. 22

GIVENS, Patrick & Elizabeth Brooks-NO DATE, but bet. Nov. 23 & 26, 1851-p. 39

GLEESON, James & Mary Grissom-Apr. 27, 1857-p. 55

GLEESON, Pleasant & Nancy Moore-Oct. 18, 1848-p. 30

GLEESON, Rufus G. & Sophronia Young-Apr. 19, 1848, by Rev. Jesse E. Hickman-p.28

GLEESON, Thos. E. & Mary Young-Dec. 4, 1849, by Rev. Wm. Jared-p. 33

GLENN, Geo. W. & Martha Jane Stockton-July 11, 1852, by Levi Jarvis, Esq.-p. 41

GLENN, James & Pheby Denton-Mar. 15, 1849, by Rev. Ozias Denton-p. 31

GLENN, John & Miss Jane Price-Feb. 16, 1848, by Rev. Wm. Goodwin-p. 28

GLENN, John & (?)Sara Denton-Oct. 4, 1850-p. 35

GLENN, John C. & Nancy Baker-Feb. 6, 1856, by Rev. M. Y. Brockett-p. 52

GLENN, John W. & Margaret A. Irwin-Mar. 20, 1856, by Rev. M. W. McConnell-p. 53

GLENN, Joseph W. & Martha W. Glenn-Dec. 21, 1843, by Jesse M. Sullivan, Esq.-p.16

GLENN, Levi & Martha Denton-Apr. 28, 1850, by J. L. Grissom, Esq.-p. 34

GLENN, Robt. & Nancy Denton-June 24, 1849, by J. L. Grissom, Esq.-p. 32

GLENN, Samuel R. & Mary Ann Franklin-Feb. 23, 1853-p. 44

GLENN, Singleton C. & Rachel Norris-Aug. 10, 1847, by Rev. Arnold Moss-p. 26

GLOVER, John H. (F.M.C.) & Frances E. Woodson(F.W.C.)-Dec. 23, 1858, by M. C.
    Dibrell, Esq.-p. 59

GODARD, M. M. & Sarah Denton-Dec. 27, 1849, by Rev. Isaac Denton-p. 33

GODDARD, Robert A. & Susan Teaters-Sept. 12, 1844, by Rev. Ozias Denton-p. 18

GOLDEN, Elijah & (?)Sian Stewart-Aug. 7, 1856, by David Snodgrass, Esq.-p. 53

GOLDEN, Elijah L. & Martha Fox (Not returned)-Feb. 26, 1842-p. 13

GOLDEN, Enoch, Jr. & Sarah Weaver-Oct. 23, 1853, by David Snodgrass, Esq.-p. 46

GOLDEN, Enoch, Sr. & (?)Malitha Fox-Oct. 29, 1848, by David Snodgrass, Esq.-p.30

GOLDEN, Enoch J. & Jane Fox-(not returned)-Mar. 23, 1842-p. 13

GOLDEN, Gideon H. & Nancy Fox-Feb. 18, 1850-p. 34

GOLDEN, Hiram B. & Nancy Stwart-(not returned)-Dec. 23, 1841-p. 12

GOLLEYHAM, Thos. & Mary Parish-July 3, 1846, by Robt. Hitchcock-p. 23

GOOCH, James & Nancy Scurlock-Aug. 2, 1858-p. 58

GOOCH, John Anderson & Sarah Short-June 30, 1856-p. 53

GOOCH, Wm. A. & Alvira Dyer-Mar. 24, 1854, by Rev. M. W. McConnell-p. 47

GOOD, James J. & Lydia Marcum-Dec. 23, 1840, by James Knowles, Esq.-p. 10

GOODALL, John L. & Jane M. Simpson-May 11, 1842, by Rev. J. E. Hickman-p. 13

GOODSON, Andrew & Lotty Little-Dec. 23, 1847-p. 27

GOOD[W?]IN, Alexander M. & Martha Ann Jones-Jan. 12, 1841, by Thos. Jones, Esq.-p. 10

GOODWIN, Marion & Myra Howard-Apr. 14, 1853, by Wm. Jared, M.G.-p. 44

GOODWIN, Thomas & Matilda Howard-Dec. 7, 1848, by Wm. Goodwin, M.G.-p. 30

GOODWIN, Wm., Jr. & Celina Jones-Dec. 27, 1849, by Rev. Wm. Goodwin-p. 33

GOOLSBY, Isaac A. & Elizabeth January-Aug. 3, 1840-p. 9

GOOLSBY, Martin & Sally Barr-July 16, 1843, by Samuel Ussery, Esq.-p. 15

GOOLSBY, Wm. & Nancy Ridge-Apr. 23, 1846, by Rev. Levi Perkins-p. 23

GRACEY, Hugh & Ann Hitchcock-Aug. 18, 1835-(L.P.-B.V.)

GRACEY, Hugh & Anny Foster-Apr. 9, 1844-p. 17

GRACY, James B. & Amanda Jones-Oct. 22, 1858, by Rev. M. W. McConnell-p. 59

GRAHAM, _____ & Elizabeth S. Lowell-July 24, 1838, by Rev. Ozias Denton-p. 2

GRAHAM, Archibald & Harriett Jane Lowell-Sept. 26, 1849-p. 32

GRAHAM, David & Elizabeth James-Feb, 14, 1852, by Rev. Wm. Burden-p. 40

GRAHAM, George & Fanny Moore-Dec. 16, 1846-p. 24

GRAHAM, John & Alevier Graham-(not returned.)-July 4, 1842-p. 13

GRAHAM, Thos. & Mary L. Call-Nov. 21, 1846-p. 24

GRAHAM, Westley & Loranny Henry-Jan. 7, 1839-p. 4

GRAHAM, Wm. & Margaret Cunningham-Feb. 2, 1841, by Wm. Green, Esq.-p. 10

GRAHAM, Wm. R. & Marylene McCormick-Feb. 23, 1840, by Anderson S. Rogers-p. 7

GRANT, Wm. & Patsy Rigsby-Dec. 2, 1846-p. 24

GRAVES, Henry & Jane Broyles-Aug. 11, 1846, by David Snodgrass-p. 23

GRAVES, R. M. C. & Elizabeth W. Walker-Oct. 30, 1850, by Rev. Miles W. McConnell-p. 36

GREEN, John A. & Lydia Caroline Williamson-Sept. 8, 1853, by Rev. Thos. E. Hutson-p. 45

GREEN, John F. & Jane E. Doyle-May 3, 1854, by Rev. James Herd-p. 48

GREEN, Lewis & Mary Ann Bray-Dec. 24, 1852-p. 43

GREEN, Robt. H. & Kitty Bruster-Sept. 30, 1856, by Rev. Wm. Jared-p. 54

GREEN, Thos. J. & Catharine M. Sorell-Feb. 15, 1844, by Rev. Abel Hutson-p. 17

GREEN, William & Mary Fryer-1820-[Ref: NSDAR #249907.]

GREEN, William W. & Roda J. Mennefee-Apr. 21, 1840, by Geo. Defrees, Esq.-p. 8

GREEN, Woodson P. & Arthusa Randals-Sept. 30, 1855, by Rev. Francis M. Hickman-p. 51

GREENE, William Graham & Louisa Hurt White-Mar. 31, 1837-[Ref: HISTORY of MENARD and MASON COUNTIES, ILLINOIS, pp. 709-714.]

GREENFIELD, Samuel & Nancy F. Knowles-Nov. 25, 1851, by Rev. T. E. Hutson-p. 39

GREENFIELD, Wm. & Elizabeth Blackburn-Feb. 25, 1841, by James Knowles, Esq.-p.10

GREER, John M. & Martha Doyle-Nov. 11, 1858, by Rev. James Herd-p. 59

GREER, Wm. F. & Cynthia C. Hill-Nov. 7, 1852, by Jas. H. Morgan-p. 43

GREGORY, Wm. & Charity Grantham-Dec. 19, 1843-p. 17

GRIFFITH, John & Nancy Dalton-Apr. 6, 1839, by Jas. T. Hayes, Esq.-p. 5

GRIFFITH, Wm. R. & Susannah Walling-Mar. 19, 1840, by Thos. Green, Esq.-p. 8

GRISSOM, Geo. A. & Laminda P. Little-June 25, 1855, by Rev. Isaac Denton-p. 50

GRISSOM, John L. & Margaret Gleeson-June 24, 1851, by Creed A. Taylor, Esq.-p.38

GRISSOM, Moses S. & Rebecca T. Irwin-June 12, 1839, by Jas. T. Hayes-p. 5

GRONER, H. C. & Martha Meredith-Jan. 13, 1841, by Robt. H. McManus, Esq.-p. 10

GUNTER, Jesse J. & Arleave Prator-June 18, 1842, by Wm. Green, Esq.-p. 13

HAILEY, Joel & Polly Earles-May 16, 1851, by Creed A. Taylor, Esq.-p. 38

HALE, Peter & Sarah Manning-Nov. 8, 1838, by Asa Certain-p. 3

HALE, Samuel (or, Lemuel?)G. & Mary Jane Walker-Aug. 16, 1854, by Rev. J. H. Morgan-p. 48

HALL, Andrew J. & T[abitha] Attaline [Adeline] Green-May 13, 1849, by Wm. Jared-p. 31. [She was dau. of Wm. & Mary (Fryer) Green.]

HALL, Andrew J. & Frances Pope-Dec. 31, 1850-p. 36

HALL, Andrew J. & Frances Pope-June 24, 1852-p. 41

HALL, Andrew J. & Julia Stewart-Jan. 28, 1851, by Rev. M. Y. Brockett-p. 37

HALL, Harrison & Lacy Mason-Oct. 10, 1838, by Wm. Knowles, Esq.-p. 3

HALTERMAN, John & Mary Ann Sevier-Nov. 20, 1813-(L.P.-B.V.)

HALTERMAN, John S. & Mary Holder-July 23, 1840, by Rev. John A. Jones-p. 9

HAMBLIN, Peter & Elizabeth Williams-Jan. 21, 1840, by A. S. Rogers-p. 7

HAMPTON, George P. & Elizabeth Price-Sept. 26, 1839, by George Defrees, Esq.-p.6

HAMPTON, Jonathan L. & Cynthia L. Lavender-Jan. 19, 1840, by Sims Dearing, Esq.-p. 7

HAMPTON, Thos. D. & Elizabeth James-Apr. 30, 1857, by Wm. Clayton, Esq.-p. 55

HAMPTON, Wm. & Sarah Ann Morris-June 10, 1852, by A. Graham-p. 41

HANCOCK, Juble B. & Sophia Mitchell-Aug. 28, 1817-(L.P.-B.V.)

HARLOW, Barney & Nancy Henseley-Dec. 12, 1843, by Anderson S. Rogers, Esq.-p.16

HARLOW, John & Margarett Lowry-Sept. 28, 1841, by Rev. James H. Morgan-p. 12

HARNESS, Wm. & Sarah Spurr-Apr. 8, 1847-p. 25

HARP, Joseph M. & Ruth Lee-Sept. 30, 1850-p. 35

HARPENDING, John W. & Sarah A. Eastland-Sept. 21, 1843, by Rev. Jesse E. Hickman-p. 16

HARRIS, Barnett & Nancy Lay-Mar. 30, 1839, by Thomas Green, Esq.-p. 4

HARRIS, Thomas C. & Mary Servel-Oct. 24, 1843, by Elijah W. Denton, Esq.-p. 16

HARRISON, Barnabas & Emily Harrison-Nov. 11, 1851, by Robt. Hitchcock-p. 39

HARRISON, David Crockett & Susannah Hill-Feb. 15, 1857, by Rich. Simpson, Esq.-
    p. 55

HARRISON, John & Mary Kelly-Aug. 30, 1855, by Zachariah Hitchcock, Esq.-p. 51

HARRISON, Montgomery & Emily Manerva Underwood-Oct. 28, 1852, by Jo. Gist, Esq.-
    p. 42

HARRISON, Rankin & Eliza Kerr-July 16, 1844-p. 18

HARRISON, Soloman & Elizabeth Hunter-Mar. 6, 1844, by Robt. H. McManus, Esq.-
    p. 17

HARRISON, Wise & Wincy Roberson-May 22, 1853, by D. Snodgrass-p. 44

HASH, Jackson & Nancy Hudgens-Oct. 23, 1840, by Wm. Hudgens, Esq.-p. 10

HASH, John W. & Nancy Franks-Oct. 13, 1842, by John Swindle, Esq.-p. 14

HASTAIN, Daniel McCumskey & Anna Green-1827-[Ref: NSDAR #108279.]

HAYSE, James T. & Mary E. Dinges-Oct. 21, 1851, by Rev. R. R. Richey-p. 39

HAYSE, Reuben & Nancy Hefner-Jan. 25, 1849, by A. J. Sims, Esq.-p. 31

HEIFNER, David & Elizabeth Broyles-Oct. 5, 1854, by John Willhite, Esq.-p. 49

HEIFNER, James D. & Parasetta Simril-Aug. 8, 1857-p. 56

HELTON, Wm. R. & Roxy Ann McGowan-June 7, 1853, by Levi Jarvis, Esq.-p. 45

HEMBREE, Andrew J. & Leale Elizabeth Jacobs-Aug. 8, 1844, by Rev. Peter Burum-
    p. 18

HEMBREE, John L. & Mary Speck-May 21, 1854, by Wm. E. Camp, Esq.-p. 48

HENRY, Andrew & Elizabeth Suttle-Jan. 27, 1848, by Rev. Thos. Stone-p. 27

HENRY, George W. & Elizabeth Stamps-Dec. 14, 1853, by Rev. Abraham Ford-p. 46

HENRY, Joseph & Rhody Netherton-Sept. 10, 1837-(L.P.-B.V.)

HENRY, Legard & Nancy _____-Sept. 11, 1838, by Asa Certain, Esq.-p. 2

HENRY, Waman L. & Elizabeth Parker-Jan. 18, 1855, by Rev. Thos. Stone-p. 49

HENRY, Wm. & Clementine B. H. Wisdom-Nov. 15, 1849, by Rev. Thos. Stone-p. 33

HENSLEY, John & Sarah Herd-Sept. 20, 1854, by Wm. Clayton, Esq.-p. 49

HENSLEY, John A. & Mary Underwood-July 6, 1840-p. 9

HENSLEY, Obadiah & Elizabeth Jane Mason-Dec. 23, 1841, by James Knowles, Esq.-
p. 12

HERD, Comodoor P. & Pheby Walling-Apr. 9, 1844-p. 17

HERD, Crockett & Mary E. Smith-Mar. 9, 1856, by Rev. James H. Morgan-p. 53

HERD, James, Senr. & Ruthy Felton-Dec. 4, 1842, by Rev. Ozias Denton, p. 14

HERD, James R. & Lucinda A. Dibrell-June 25, 1840, by Rev. John A. Jones-p. 9

HERD, James V. & Sarah E. Holland-Feb. 5, 1856, by Creed A. Taylor, Esq.-p. 52

HERD, John B. & Louisa Keithley-Feb. 17, 1842, by A. S. Rogers, Esq.-p. 13

HERD, Joseph S.[or, L.?] & Cynthia M. Smith-Dec. 21, 1854, by Rev. Jas. Herd-p.49

HERD, Joseph W. & Sarah E. Doyle-Aug. 13, 1846, by Rev. Isaac Denton-p. 23

HERD, Joseph W. & Nancy E. Green-Aug. 27, 1854, by C. A. Taylor, Esq.-p. 48

HERD, Lawson & Anna Narcissa Hunter-June 12, 1848, by Wm. Clayton, Esq.-p. 29

HERRON, Robt. & Mary Ann Whitfield-May 24, 1849, by Rev. Levi Perkins-p. 31

HESTER, John H. & Margaret Bryant-May 8, 1857, by R. Simpson, Esq.-p. 56

HEWITT, Alexander & Emila Carrick-Sept. 14, 1847-p. 26

HICKEY, Cornelius & Eliza J. Brown-Sept. 1, 1842, by Wm. Glenn, Esq.-p. 14

HICKEY, Isaac Newton & Nancy A. Frost-Aug. 21, 1855, by John Crook, Esq.-p. 51

HICKEY, Joshua & Mary Jane Jones-Mar. 24, 1847-p. 25

HICKEY, Wm. & Lucy Jane Howell-Apr. 8, 1855, by Zach. Hitchcock, Esq.-p. 50

HICKS, Jesse & Rachel Hughs-Nov. 12, 1846-p. 24

HILL, James A. & Huldy Greer-Dec. 30, 1847, by James Herd, M.G.-p. 27

HILL, Joab & Mrs. Elizabeth Pinner-Feb. 28, 1839, by Rev. Ozias Denton-p. 4

HILL, John & Maniza Holmes-July 21, 1853, by Rev. M. W. McConnell-p. 45

HILL, Wm. A. & Louisa Howard-June 4, 1840, by Thomas Green, Esq.-p. 9

HILTON, Leroy & Nancy McGowan-Nov. 16, 1845, by Rev. Arnold Moss-p. 21

HINESLY, James M. & Mila Hamilton-Feb. 21, 1851, by Abram Saylors, Esq.-p. 37

HINKLE, Isaac & Martha Holland-Dec. 28, 1841, by Anderson/Rogers, Esq.-p. 12

HITCHCOCK, Benjamin & Sarah An Byers-Aug. 24, 1848, by Robt. Hitchcock, Esq.-p.29

HITCHCOCK, Elijah & Mary Bushears-Mar. 13, 1847-p. 25

HITCHCOCK, Elisha & Margarett E. Sherrell-Dec. 11, 1849-p. 33

HITCHCOCK, Wm. C. & Nancy Lafever-Nov. 3, 1848, by Robt. Hitchcock, Esq.-p. 30

HITCHCOCK, Wm. L. & Rutha Carland-Aug. 3, 1844, by Robt. Hitchcock, Esq.-p. 18

HITCHCOCK, Wm. L. & Elizabeth Carland-May 3, 1857, by Z. Hitchcock, Esq.-p. 55

HOLDER, Andrew J. & Jane Holder-Aug. 12, 1841, by Matthias Hutson, Esq.-p. 11

HOLDER, Fielding & Lydia Payne [or, Pogue?]-June 5, 1838, by Rev. Ozias Denton-p. 2

HOLDER, Joel & Charlotta Howard-Mar. 26, 1845-p. 19

HOLDER, Spencer, Sr. & Elizabeth Nichols-Apr. 28, 1841, by Thos. Green, Esq.-p.11

HOLLAND, Harrison M. & Pamela Doyle-Oct. 24, 1845, by Rev. James Herd-p. 21

HOLLAND, Jackson A. & Mary A. Hunter-Dec. 5, 1848, by Rev. Wm. Burden-p. 30

HOLLAND, James R. & Elizabeth A. Pollard-Aug. 20, 1846, by Rev. Arnold Moss-p.23

HOLLAND, Jesse L. & Malvina Doyle-Feb. 11, 1841, by Thos. Green, Esq.-p. 10

HOLLAND, Presley & Mary Little-Aug. 4, 1843, by Rev. James H. Morgan-p. 15

HOLLAND, Seaborn & Elizabeth Holder-Sept. 27, 1838, by Thos. Green, Esq.-p. 3

HOLLAND, Seabo[r]n & Charlotte Cope-Apr. 3, 1855, by Rev. James Herd-p. 50

HOLMAN, Albert J. & Jane Speers-May 21, 1840, by David Snodgrass, Esq.-p. 8

HOLMAN, Z.[or, B.?] B. & Mary Ann Hitchcock-Sept. 26, 1854, by David Snodgrass, Esq.-p. 49

HOLMES, Alphonso L. & Mary E. Lowrey-Aug. 12, 1851, by Rev. W. G. Chonnley-p. 38

HOLTON, Wm. & Julia Ann B. Bailey-Oct. 19, 1843, by Rev. Jesse Cole-p. 16

HOOPER, David & Louisa Catherine Gray-July 9, 1855, by M. C. Dibrell, Esq.-p. 50

HOOPER, James & Mary Ogden-June 27, 1852, by Wm. Clayton, Esq.-p. 41

HOOTEN, Littleton & Lincinda Bradford-Nov. 8, 1850, by Rev. Thos. Stone-p. 36

HOOVER, Wm. W. & Harriet Harbrough-Feb. 20, 1855, by Rev. F. M. Hickman-p. 50

HOPKINS, Isaac & Mary Rawlings-July 8, 1838, by John Gillentine, Esq.-p. 2

HOPKINS, James & Mary Williams-Dec. 24, 1838, by John Gillentine, Esq.-p. 4

HORN, Albert & Jane Johnson-Nov. 8, 1838, by David Snodgrass-p. 3

HORTEN [HOOTEN], Martin & Sarah Charles-Nov. 26, 1846, by Rev. Thos. E. Hutson-p. 24

HOWARD, _____ P. & Jarusha Stephens-Mar. 9, 1848, by James Jackson, Esq.-p. 28

HOWARD, A. S. & Mary C. Taylor-Oct. 10, 1857, by Wm. Clayton, Esq.-p. 56

HOWARD, Frederick N. & Myra McConnell-Sept. 1, 1842, by Rev. J.E. Hickman-p. 14

HOWARD, Geo. D. & Mrs. Jane Pinner-June 24, 1835-(L.P.-B.V.)

HOWARD, James & Julia A. Broyles-June 14, 1855, by Rev. Levi Perkins-p. 50

HOWARD, James D. & Nancy Bowman-Dec. 12, 1838, by Levi Perkins, M.G.-p. 4

HOWARD, John & Rhoda Lundy-Dec. 5, 1849-p. 33

HOWARD, John & Susan Matilda Southard-Jan. 2, 1856, by D.M. Southard, Esq.-p.52

HOWARD, Nathan B. & Sarah Whitson-May 18, 1838-p. 2

HOWARD, Nathan B. & Sarah Whitson-July 25, 1839, by Rev. Josiah Williams-p. 5

HOWARD, Wm. & Malinda Haston-Sept. 5, 1839, by John Gillentine, Esq.-p. 6

HOWARD, Wm. & Elizabeth Nicholas-Nov. 1, 1852-p. 42

HOWARD, Wm. P. & Mary Goodwin-Dec. 29, 1849-p. 33

HOWARD, Wm. S. & Nancy Farley-Dec. 28, 1846-p. 25

HOWELL, Aandrew & Celia Lafevers-Mar. 19, 1857, by Rev. Levi Perkins-p. 55

HOWELL, Isaac & Jincy Elvira Bussell-June 5, 1838, by Rev. Levi Perkins-p. 2

HOWELL, John H. & Catharine Hyder-Mar. 24, 1842, by Wm. Glenn, Esq.-p. 13

HOWELL, Joseph H. & Angeline E. Hunter-Nov. 4, 1841, by Wm. R. Tucker, Esq.-p.12

HOWELL, Lewis & Jerusha Duncan-Dec. 19, 1848, by Abe Saylor, Esq.-p. 30

HOWELL, Silas & Matilda C. Rice-Mar. 21, 1843-p. 15

HOWELL, Tilman & Ann Sherrell-Apr. 6, 1856, by Rev. Levi Perkins-p. 53

HOWLETTE, John & Agnes Scarborough-Mar. 23, 1858, by C. S. Eastland, Esq.-p. 57

HUDDLESTON, David & Mary Lollar-Dec. 20, 1846, by Rev. John B. Poniter-p. 24

HUDDLESTON, David F. & Arey L. Lollar-Nov. 20, 1845, by Shadrick Price, Esq.-p.21

HUDDLESTON, John & Mary Savage-Sept. 9, 1843-p. 16

HUDDLESTON, Wm. P. & Elizabeth Dyer-Aug. 8, 1856, by Rev. M. W. McConnell-p. 53

HUDGENS, Crockett & Lucinda Fisk-Oct. 17, 1850, by Wm. Jared-p. 35

HUDGENS, Hampton & Eliza Waller-Jan. 20, 1842, by Anderson S. Rogers, Esq.-p. 13

HUDGENS, Shelby & Mary Austin-Feb. 22, 1839, by Anderson S. Rogers-p. 4

HUDSON [or, HUTSON], Wm. H. & Nancy Farley-Aug. 31, 1843, by John Wilhite, Esq.-
       p. 16

HUGHES, Henry F. & Nancy Wilhite-Apr. 5, 1846, by Solomon Yeager, Esq.-p. 23

HUGHS, Samuel & Polly Holman-Jan. 10, 1841, by David Snodgrass, Esq.-p. 10

HUMPHREYS, Benjamin & Rachael Knowles-Oct. 9, 1856, by Rev. Isaac Denton-p. 54

HUMPHREYS, David & Mahala Knowles-July 3, 1842, by Jas. Knowles-p. 13

HUNTER, Alson & Rosery (?)Aurs-Sept. 11, 1845, by Rev. Arnold Moss-p. 19

HUNTER, Braxton & Sarah Hunter-Mar. 14, 1839, by Wm. Little, Esq.-p. 4. [She was
       a grand-niece to Daniel Boone.]

HUNTER, Charles & Sarah Lowrey-Sept. 10, 1846-p. 23

HUNTER, Dudley & Amey Lowrey-Oct. 17, 1844-p. 18

HUNTER, James & Aryella Henry-Jan. 18, 1845, by Thos. Stone-p. 21

HUNTER, James & Alcey Thomas-Sept. 17, 1850-p. 35

HUNTER, James & Mary E. Lance-Jan. 26, 1854, by Joseph Gist, Esq.-p. 47

HUNTER, Jesse & Milly Ann White-Jan. 11, 1854, by John Madewell-p. 47

HUNTER, John & Lavina Hyder-Sept. 21, 1848, by Solomon Yeager, Esq.-p. 29

HUNTER, John & Jelina Metcalf-May 30, 1852, by Wm. C. Johnson, Esq.-p. 41

HUNTER, Joseph & Miss Martha Bohanon-Nov. 27, 1845, by Rev. Thos. Stone-p. 21
[Is this a double wedding? See: James B. Lowrey.]

HUNTER, Lenias F. & Martha Green-Feb. 10, 1852-p. 40

HUNTER, Turner L. & Elizabeth Ann Holland-Mar. 29, 1848, by M.C. Dibrell, Esq.-
p. 28

HURT, Obadiah & Mary E. Taylor-Feb. 19, 1847-p. 25

HUTCHENS, Geo. W. C. & Mary Dildine-July 4, 1844, by Thos. Jones, Esq.-p. 18

HUTCHINGS, Charles & Jane Hutchings-Feb. 5, 1843, by Jesse M. Sullivan, Esq.-
p. 15. [Is this a double wedding? See: John G. Elkins.]

HUTCHINGS, Francis & Arminda Moore-July 15, 1858, by J. L. Grissom, Esq.-p. 58

HUTCHINGS, Thos. J. & Sarah Cooper-Aug. 21, 1850, by Rev. V. V. Richey-p. 35

HUTCHINGS, Wm. & Lucinda A. C. Davis-Jan. 28, 1856-p. 52

HUTCHINGS, Wm. C. & Paulina L. J. Robbins-Aug. 12, 1850-p. 35

HUTSON, Abel C. & Sarah Howard-Jan. 22, 1846, by Rev. Thos. E. Hutson-p. 21
[Is this a double wedding? See: Jonathan P. Lane.]

HUTSON, Archibald & Nancy Oliver-Oct. 14, 1845, by Rev. Abel Hutson-p. 21

HUTSON, David & Nancy Stewart-Sept. 25, 1839, by Asa Certain, Esq.-p. 6

HUTSON, David & Mary Bussell-Jan. 19, 1842, by Wm. Glenn, Esq.-p. 13

HUTSON, Geo. W. & Milly Farley-Mar. 7, 1848, by John Wilhite, Esq.-p. 28

HUTSON, Geo. W. & Amarinda Hutchings-Sept. 16, 1854, by J. L. Grissom, Esq.-p.49

HUTSON, Geo. Willoughby & Nancy Johnson-Nov. 8, 1857, by Wm. I. Russell, Esq.-
p. 56

HUTSON, Isaiah, Sr. & Elizabeth Knowles-Mar. 11, 1857, by Rev. Thos. E. Hutson-
p. 55

HUTSON, Isaiah A. & Sarah H. Hutchings-May 5, 1850, by J.L. Grissom, Esq.-p. 34

HUTSON, Isaih & Brittania Holder-Aug. 11, 1845, by I. H. Graham, Esq.-p. 19

HUTSON, Jesse Herd & Zilpha W. J. Jarnagin-Sept. 7, 1856, by James A. Knowles,
Esq.-p. 54

HUTSON, Matthias, Jr. & Amy Jane Green-Feb. 14, 1843, by Robt. H. McManus, Esq.-
p. 15. [She was dau. of Avery Green.]

HUTSON, Pleasant & Margarett J. Pirtle-Mar. 8, 1848, by John Wilhite, Esq.-p. 28

HUTSON, Reuben P. & Serona Wiggins-Feb. 15, 1857, by Jas. A. Knowles, Esq.-p. 55

HUTSON, Rouben & Sarah Swindle-June 20, 1852, by Rev. T. E. Hutson-p. 41

HUTSON, Silas & Nancy Smith-Oct. 28, 1847, by David Fruyshurd, M.G.-p. 27

HUTSON, William & Elizabeth McEwin-Sept. 26, 1839, by Asa Certain, Esq.-p. 6

HUTSON, Wm. C. & Julina Chisom-Sept. 9, 1856, by Rev. Jeremiah Webb-p. 54

HUTSON, Wm. H. [See: HUDSON]

HUTSON, Wm. H. & Ellen D. Irwin-Oct. 18, 1849, by Rev. Wm. Jared-p. 32

HYDER, James & Ruth Alexander-Sept. 26, 1844, by Solomon Yeager, Esq.-p. 18

IPOCH, Enoch & Sarah Busy-Dec. 15, 1838-p. 4

IPOCH, Enoch & Elizabeth Savage-June 12, 1841-(not returned)-p. 11. [Was she dau. of Kenall Savage?]

IPOCK, Bryant & Rebecca Robinson-Oct. 10, 1844-p. 18

IRWIN, Isaac N. & Lorina S. Taylor-Dec. 3, 1846, by Wm. Glenn, Esq.-p. 24

IRWIN, Wm. & Susannah Flinchum-Apr. 10, 1840, by Rev. S. G. Buxton-p. 8

ISBELL, James & Malvina Mitchell-Feb. 27, 1851, by Rev. Levi Perkins-p. 37

ISHAM, Geo. W. & Susan Kirk-Apr. 1, 1841, by Rev. J. H. Morgan-p. 11

ISHAM, James H. & Vilette Cash-Aug. 29, 1839, by Rev. Corder Stone-p. 5

JACKSON, Geo. F. & Ruth Graves-Aug. 17, 1854, by Rev. M. Y. Brockett-p. 48

JACKSON, Thos. & Matilda (?)Davy-Oct. 1, 1846-p. 24

JACKSON, Wm. & Rebecca Dixon-Feb. 17, 1852, by John Madewell, Esq.-p. 40

JARNIGAN, Jas. P. & Jane Knowles-May 7, 1856, by Rev. T. E. Hutson-p. 53

JARVIS, Alexander & Susan Jane Franklin-Jan. 20, 1858-p. 57

JARVIS, Foster R. & Mahala J. Little-Oct. 16, 1853, by Wm. I. Russell, Esq.-p.46

JARVIS, Jesse & Rachael D. Stewart-Nov. 10, 1853, by A. J. Sims, Esq.-p. 46

JARVIS, Sylvester & Maranda Simril-July 14, 1858, by Rev. Thos. E. Hutson-p. 58

JAY, Wm. & Nancy Whitson-June 17, 1841-(not returned)-p. 11

JERNIGAN, Wiley & Sarah Short-Apr. 19, 1856-p. 53

JETT, John W. & Arabella Downey-Nov. 25, 1856, by James Herd, Esq.-p. 54

JETT, Thomas J. & Elizabeth Turner-Oct. 7, 1858, by Rev. Wm. Jared-p. 58

JOHNSON, _____ & Mary H. England-Dec. 6, 1838, by Jesse E. Hickman-p. 3

JOHNSON, Absalom & Betty Vass-Apr. 12, 1858-p. 57

JOHNSON, Henry B. & Henrietta Lollar-(not ret. but did m.)-Aug. 4, 1841-p. 11

JOHNSON, James & Milly Roberts-Dec. 23, 1855, by Rev. Isaac C. Woodward-p. 52

JOHNSON, John & Olley Broyles-Dec. 14, 1853, by Rev. Wm. Jared-p. 46

JOHNSON, John R. & Louisa Bounds-Aug. 23, 1849, by Rev. Thos. Stone-p. 32

JOHNSON, Jonathan & Sarah Mars-June 16, 1850, by Wm. Clayton-p. 34

JOHNSON, Stokely D. & Matilda Cope-Sept. 22, 1853, by Rev. James Herd-p. 46

JOHNSON, Wm. & Polly Weaver-Dec. 1, 1841, by David Snodgrass-p. 12

JOHNSON, Wm. C. & Mary Ann Carmichael-Jan. 3, 1839, by David Snodgrass-p. 4

JOHNSTON, Andrew & Jane Gracey-June 10, 1846-p. 23

JOHNSTON, Carrol & Rebecca Anderson-May 13, 1846, by Thos. Jones, Esq.-p. 23

JOHNSTON, Westely & Mary Ann Bozearth-May 10, 1847-p. 25

JONES, Allen & Caroline Holder-Jan. 10, 1843, by Elijah W. Denton-p. 14

JONES, Edenton & Jane Wisdom-Nov. 14, 1844, by Jesse Hickman-p. 18

JONES, Henderson M. & Elizabeth A. Gracy-Jan. 25, 1846, by Rev. Miles W. McConnell-p. 22

JONES, Henderson M. & Elizabeth McConnell-Oct. 19, 1852-p. 42

JONES, Henry H. & Mary Howard-June 10, 1846, by Joseph Gist, Esq.-p. 23

JONES, Irwin & Elizabeth E. Price-July 12, 1852, by Rev. Wm. Jared-p. 41

JONES, James & Tabitha Charles-Oct. 18, 1840, by Wm. Knowles, Esq.-p. 9

JONES, James & Eady Sparkman-Dec. 31, 1851, by C. A. Taylor, Esq.-p. 40

JONES, James C. & Martha George-July 29, 1845, by Rev. Nathan Judd-P. 19

JONES, James R. & Maria L. Martin-May 6, 1841, by Thomas Jones-p. 11

JONES, Jefferson & Brunetta Cameron-Sept. 18, 1842, by Wm. Glenn, Jr., Esq.-p.14

JONES, John & Susan Paulston-Dec. 21, 1857, by Wm. I. Russell, Esq.-p. 57

JONES, Madson F. & Selia Howell-Sept. 5, 1844, by Alvey Bussell, Esq.-p. 18

JONES, Monroe & Jane Meredith-Sept. 14, 1845, by Jesse E. Hickman-p. 19

JONES, Monroe & Sarah Pearson-Dec. 4, 1851-p. 39

JONES, Pleasant & Eleanor Caroline Hathaway-July 15, 1854-p. 48

JONES, Richard Douglass & Elizabeth Weaver-Feb. 8, 1849, by Abram Saylors, Esq.-
p. 31

JONES, Thomas & Frances Mitchell-Dec. 24, 1850, by Rev. Levi Perkins-p. 36

JONES, Thomas, Sr. & Susannah Duncan-Jan. 3, 1858, by Wm. I. Russell, Esq.-p. 57

JONES, Thos. J. & Mary Elizabeth Stiles-Mar. 4, 1856, by Rev. Jesse G. Rice-p.53

JONES, Wiley B. & Nancy Ann Burgess-Oct. 2, 1844-p. 18

JONES, Wm. & Mary M. T. Little-May 1, 1847-p. 25

JONES, Wm. C. & Mary Holder-Dec. 19, 1839, by Jesse Walling, Esq.-p. 7

JONES, Wm. M. & Catharine P. Hale-Jan. 18, 1852, by Wm. Clayton, Esq.-p. 40

JONES, Wm. Zach. & Margaret Ann Stiles-July 5, 1855, by M. C. Dibrell, Esq.-p.50

JONES, Zechariah & Mary Bennett-Feb. 26, 1846, by Jesse M. Sullivan, Esq.-p. 22
    [She was dau. of Walker Bennett.]

JUDD, John & Abigail Lee-Oct. 15, 1854, by Rev. S. B. Lyles-p. 49

JULIN, Washington & Martha Kirk-Mar. 26, 1840, by Rev. Stephen G. Buxton-p. 8

KEATHLEY, Thos. J. & Almeady Smith-Dec. 7, 1853, by Rev. Isaac C. Woodward-p. 46

KEATHLY, Martin & Emily Crain-May 31, 1858, by Rev. J. L. Brown-p. 58

KEATHLY, Wm. H. & Sarah Webb-Feb. 12, 1857, by Rev. Thos. E. Hutson-p. 55

KEATHLY, Willis & Eliza Ann Green-Mar. 6, 1855, by Rev. Thos. E. Hutson-p. 50

KEITHLEY, Andrew C. & Martha White-Nov. 3, 1840-p. 9. [She was dau. of John &
    Adelphia (Doyle) White, Jr.]

KEITHLEY, Joseph A. & Martha Herd-Nov. 25, 1841, by Thos. Green, Esq.-p. 12

KEITHLEY, Willis & Mary Ann Driver-Feb. 9, 1847-p. 25

KELLEY, Thos. R. & Elizabeth Certain-Dec. 22, 1840, by Rev. S. G. Buxton-p. 10

KELLY, George & Martha J. Eastland-Nov. 17, 1847, by Joseph B. Wyns, M.G.-p. 27

KELLY James C. & Mrs. Mary Jane Carroll-Dec. 17, 1838, by Asa Certain, Esq.-p. 4

KEMMER, Andrew R. & Elizabeth H. Crook-NO DATE, but bet. Mar. 29 & Apr. 13, 1853-
p. 44

KENNDY, Thos. F. & Mary C. Allen-Jan. 19, 1849, by Wm. Clayton, Esq.-p. 31

KERBY, John & Mary Barclay-Apr. 25, 1855, by David Snodgrass, Esq.-p. 50

KERBY, Laban & Hannah Miller-Dec. 24, 1856, by M. C. Dibrell, Esq.-p. 55

KERBY, Reuben & Milly Kerby-Feb. 14, 1853, by Wm. R. Tucker, Esq.-p. 44

KERBY, Wm. & Sarah Webster-July 12, 1854, by Rev. Wm. Jared-p. 48

KERR, John D. & Nancy Kirk-Feb. 18, 1844, by James H. Morgan, ECC-p. 17

KERR, Jonathan R. & Jane Brown-Feb. 5, 1853, by Wm. R. Tucker, Esq.-p. 44

KERR, Joseph, Jr. & Elizabeth Bradley-Dec. 3, 1838, by Geo. Defrees, Esq.-p. 3

KEY, Wm. & Louisa Southard-Aug. 12, 1838, by Rev. John Green-p. 2

KILGROW, E. W. & Martha Lollar-July 29, 1839, by Rev. Levi Perkins-p. 5. [Is
this a double wedding? See: Corder Lollar.]

KILGROW, Elias W. & Rebecca Lollar-Aug. 5, 1845, by Rev. Thos. Stone-p. 22

KING, Robt. & Ann Roberson-June 26, 1852-p. 41

KING, Sam'l. B. & Mary Jane Dunn-Jan. 22, 1854, by Rev. Thos. Hutson-p. 47

KINNARD, John & Polly Parker-May 13, 1838, by Rev. Corder Stone-p. 2

KIRBY, David & Agness Worley-Dec. 18, 1849-p. 33

KIRBY, Woodson P. & Ann Pearson-Feb. 15, 1844, by David Snodgrass, Esq.-p. 17

KITCHERSIDE, Chesley & Tymanda Smith-Sept. 21, 1843, by David Snodgrass, Esq.-
p. 16

KITRELL, Joseph & Anna Hutchings-May 15, 1847-p. 26

KITRELL, Wm. & Martha Taylor-Apr. 2, 1844, by Thos. Jones, Esq.-p. 17

KITRELL, Wm. S. & (?)Linney Sherrell-May 1, 1856, by Rev. L. H. Bennett-p. 53

KIZER, Wm. D. & Martha F. Bennett-Mar. 18, 1858-p. 57

KNOWLES, Cason S. & Stacey Hutchings-Aug. 13, 1850-p. 35

KNOWLES, Ellit & Cela Clark-June 21, 1849, by James Webb, Esq.-p. 32

KNOWLES, Hiram & Mary E. Gibbs-Nov. 28, 1838, by Rev. Stephen G. Buxton-p. 3

KNOWLES, James A. & Caroline Shuster-Dec. 3, 1855, by Rev. Isaac C. Woodward-p.52

KNOWLES, John & Hester C. Gibbs-Dec. 29, 1838-p. 4

KNOWLES, John & Ammalise Rascoe-Dec. 22, 1846-p. 24

KNOWLES, John W. & Malvina C. Stewart-Nov. 17, 1857-p. 56

KNOWLES, Peter B. & Anna Swindle-Aug. 26, 1852, by Rev. T. E. Hutson-p. 42

KNOWLES, Wm. & Martha Ann Rascoe-Aug. 4, 1840, by Wm. Knowles, Esq.-p. 9

KNOWLES, Wm. & Catherine Roberts-Sept. 20, 1846, by Jno. Swindle-p. 23

KNOWLES, Wm., Sr. & Susan Ann Denton-Apr. 13, 1852, by Rev. T.E. Hutson-p. 41

KUHN, James A. & Lucy Hollinsworth-Feb. 9, 1857, by Creed A. Taylor, Esq.-p. 55

LACK, Benj. & Eliza Quillen-Apr. 5, 1854, by Rev. L. H. Bennett-p. 48

LACK, Cader & Alcy Adcock-Aug. 7, 1856, by Wm. I. Russell, Esq.-p. 53

LACK, Wm. & Martha E. Lewis-May 13, 1852, by Wm. I. Russell-p. 41

LAFEVER, Geo. & Sarah Ann Trobaugh-Jan. 29, 1857, by Rev. Levi Perkins-p. 55

LAFEVER, James & Paulina Boyd-Jan. 28, 1857, by Rev. Levi Perkins-p. 55

LAFEVER, Thos. & Rachel Traubough-Jan. 26, 1850, by Robt. Hitchcock, Esq.-p. 33

LAMB, Joseph & Jane Pope-May 26, 1852, by Rev. M. Y. Brockett-p. 41

LAMB, Lawsoner & Sarah Cody-Dec. 5, 1839, by Rev. Jesse Cole-p. 7

LAMB, Yance & Mary Ann Buckner-Mar. 29, 1853, by A. F. Lawrence-p. 44

LAMBETH, Jesse & Agness Warren-Sept. 10, 1843, by Rev. David L. Mitchell-p. 16

LANCE, Geo. W. & Margaret England-Feb. 24, 1856, by Henry J. Lyda, Esq.-p. 53

LANCE, James M. & Mary Hooper-Apr. 14, 1858, by Rev. J. W. Tarrant-p. 57

LANCE, John & Mary Hickey-Dec. 17, 1849-p. 33

LANCE, Samuel & Mary McBride-June 1, 1848, by David Snodgrass, Esq.-p. 28

LANCE, Samuel & Naomi Harrison-Dec. 30, 1856, by Rev. J. B. Wynn-p. 55

LANCE, Thomas J. & Martha Anderson-Feb. 17, 1853, by Rev. James Herd-p. 44

LANE, David C. & Mary Halterman-June 21, 1842, by Rev. I. C. Woodard-p. 13

LANE, Jonathan P. & Mary Jane Hutson-Jan. 22, 1846, by Rev. Thos. E. Hutson-p.21
[Is this a double wedding? See: Abel C. Hutson.]

LANE, Richard B. & Elizabeth Halterman-May 24, 1852, by Rev. T. E. Hutson-p. 41

LANE, Turner [Jr.] & Miss Mary Scoggins-Dec. 31, 1829, by Jesse Scoggins, Esq.-
[from: SPARTONIAN & MT. DISTRICT ADVERTISER (Sparta, Tenn.), Jan. 16, 1830.
. He was b. Nov. 17, 1806; d. Dec. 8, 1872. They are buried in marked graves
in Temperanceville Cemetery, Howard Co., Ark., next to her father, who is
in an unmarked grave. She was dau. of Rev. John & Elizabeth (White) Scoggin, Jr. He was son of Revol. soldier Turner Lane, Sr. & wife Martha Anderson. Turner, Sr. stated in his Pension record that he was b. Jan. 9,
1762, Hanover Co., Va. He was m. Sept. 27, 1787, Washington Co., Va.]

LANE, W. C. & Mary A. Rogers-Jan. 16, 1855, by Wm. Clayton, Esq.-p. 49

LARGENT, James & Minerva Hunter-Feb. 8, 1843, by David Snodgrass, Esq.-p.15

LARGIN, John & Peggy Anderson-Aug. 13, 1818-(L.P.-B.V.)

LATHAM, James & Nancy Short-May 25, 1849, by Rev. Isaac Denton-p. 32

LAWRENCE, _____ W. & Cynthia C. Copeland-Dec. 9, 1840, by Rev. Abel Hutson-p.9

LAWSON, Bosby & Jane Hodge-Aug. 16, 1839, by John Gill[entine?]-p.5

LAWSON, Sherod & Mahala Henderson-Jan. 7, 1841-p. 10

LAY, Zachariah A. & Dosea E. Hooper-Mar. 1, 1840, by James Knowles, Esq.-p. 8

LEACH, James C. & Jennetta B. Willhite-July 4, 1853, by Rev. Thos. Stone-p. 45

LEDBETTER, Noah & Janetta Kidwell-Feb. 15, 1853, by Rich. Bradley, Esq.-p. 44

LEE, Jeremiah & Jane Bussell-July 17, 1854, by John Willhite, Esq.-p. 48

LEE, Wm. Jasper & Charlotte Evans-Jan. 29, 1849, by Rev. Arnold Moss-p. 31

LEFTWICH, Jefferson & Luraney C. Lisk-Aug. 30, 1854, by Rev. John A. Ellis-p. 49

LEN, Alfred & Elizabeth Stewart-Feb. 12, 1853, by Wm. C. Johnson, Esq.-p. 44

LENTZ, Geo. W. & Mary L. Brewster-Sept. 17, 1851, by Rev. M. Y. Brockett-p. 39

LEWIS, Barnet & Abigail Williams-Dec. 26, 1852, by Richmond Frasier, Esq.-p. 43

LEWIS, Barnett & Diademy Harness-Dec. 10, 1858, by Rev. J. B. Wynns-p. 59

LEWIS, Benjamin M. & Sarah Lewis-Oct. 10, 1846, by Joel Whitley, Esq.-p. 23

LEWIS, Bird & Martha Bryan-Dec. 15, 1843, by Anderson S. Rogers, Esq.-p. 16

LEWIS, David H. & Mary Brittain-Aug. 22, 1850, by Jo. G. Mitchell, Esq.-p. 35

LEWIS, Jacob & Emily Anderson-July 25, 1854, by Rev. James H. Morgan-p. 48

LEWIS, James K. Polk & Catharine Cope-Nov. 17, 1858, by Wm. I. Russell, Esq.-p.59

LEWIS, James M. & Sarah E. Copeland-Oct. 20, 1852, by Rev. T. E. Hutson-p. 42

LEWIS, James W. & Elizabeth Miller-June 29, 1852, by J. G. Mitchell, Esq.-p. 41

LEWIS, Thomas & Martha Crawley-July 12, 1840, by Anderson S. Rogers, Esq.-p. 9

LEWIS, Thos. J. & Kiza Hutchings-Apr. 16, 1854, by Wm. I. Russell, Esq.-p. 48

LEWIS, Turner & Polly Ann Rodgers-July 8, 1844-p. 18

LEWIS, Wm. & Nancy Hutchings-Apr. 16, 1849, by Rev. Dan'l. Lasiter-p. 31

LEWIS, Wm. & Artamissa Shannon-Jan. 9, 1858-p. 57

LEWIS, Wm., Jr. & Sarah Rhea-Nov. 24, 1853-p. 46

LEWIS, Wm. G. & Nancy Lewis-Mar. 6, 1851, by Rev. John Green-p. 37

LINDSEY, Eli W. & Jane Rowland-Apr. 13, 1850, by Robt. Hitchcock, Esq.-p. 34

LINDSEY, John C. W. & Elizabeth J. Rhea-Oct. 21, 1841, by Rev. Levi Perkins-p.12

LINDSEY, Wm. A. & Jane Mattock [Matlock?]-July 13, 1843, by Robt. H. McManus, Esq.-p. 15

LINN, Dommer & Jane England-Mar. 3, 1850, by Shadrick Price, Esq.-p. 34

LINNVILLE, Ammon H. & Ann Eliza Hickey-Nov. 15, 1855, by Henry J. Lyda, Esq.-p.52

LITTLE, Bryce & Martha P. Snodgrass-Feb. 22, 1843, by Wm. W. Moore, Esq.-p. 15

LITTLE, Bryce & Mrs. Rachael Wallis-Sept. 30, 1856, by M. C. Dibrell, Esq.-p. 54

LITTLE, David & Sarah Wallis-Apr. 19, 1855, by Wm. R. Tucker, Esq.-p. 50

LITTLE, Freeland S. & Rebecca England-Dec. 19, 1843, by D. Snodgrass, Esq.-p. 16

LITTLE, Harmon & Polly Simpson-Mar. 7, 1816, by Henry Neile, J.P.-(L.P.-B.V.)

LITTLE, Harmon & Nancy Teeters-Sept. 26, 1855, by Elijah W. Denton, Esq.-p. 51

LITTLE, Hiram & Sarah Cope-Oct. 12, 1848, by Rev. James Herd-p. 30

LITTLE, John & Eliza Ann Snodgrass-Dec. 19, 1839, by David Snodgrass, Esq.-p. 7

LITTLE, John & Mary Gillentine-Oct. 4, 1847-p. 27

LITTLE, Simpson & Eliza Gleeson-Oct. 24, 1838, by Joshua Mason, Esq.-p. 3

LITTLE, Thos. G. & Mary H. Wallace-Jan. 1, 1847, by Joel Whitley, Esq.-p. 25

LOLLAR, Corder & Nancy Caroline Patillar-July 29, 1839, by Rev. Levi Perkins-p.5
[Is this a double wedding? See: E. W. Kilgrow.]

LOW, Jeremiah & Lucy Jane Hart-Mar. 23, 1854, by Abram Saylors, Esq.-p. 47

LOWELL, (?)Parnn G. & Martha Worley-Dec. 12, 1840, by Wm. Little, Esq.-p. 10

LOWELL, Turner G. & Dorcas Prock-Nov. 30, 1856, by Wm. Clayton, Esq.-p. 54

LOWERY, Vance C. & Maria White-June 18, 1850, by Rev. J. B. Wynne-p. 34. [She
was dau. of Woodson Phillips & Nancy (Mitchell) White.]

LOWREY, Charles & Catharine Hudgens-Jan. 18, 1844, by Rev. Jesse E. Hickman-p.17

LOWREY, James & Henrietta Hunter-July 15, 1852, by J. D. Hyder, Esq.-p. 41

LOWREY, James B. & Elizabeth Hunter-Nov. 27, 1845, by Rev. Thos. Stone-p. 21
[Is this a double wedding? See: Joseph Hunter.]

LOWREY, John & Martha J. Taylor-Jan. 8, 1846, by Jos. G. Mitchell, Esq.-p. 22

LOWREY, John & Rose Ann Lance-Feb. 16, 1850, by Wm. Clayton, Esq.-p. 34

LOWREY, Wm. A. & Juliann M. Morgan-Dec. 9, 1847, by Rev. N. L. Murphey-p. 27

LOWRY, Mark & Amanda M. Bunch-Dec. 25, 1858, by Rev. M. Y. Brockett-p. 59

LUNDY, Daniel & Mary Hart [Hurt]-June 23, 1852, by Sam Usrey, Esq.-p. 41

LUNDY, Daniel S. & Elizabeth Wisdom-Dec. 21, 1843-p. 17

LUNY, Peter & Sarah Cummings-Sept. 25, 1846, by Rev. Daniel Lassater-P. 23

LYDA, Daniel & Amanda Meek-Jan. 16, 1851, by Andrew J. Sims, Esq.-p. 36

LYLES, Joshua & Mary Louisa Hunter-Nov. 16, 1854, by Rev. M. Y. Brockett-p. 49

LYTLE, Wm. & Sarah Dudley-Jan. 31, 1859, by Wm. E. Camp, Esq.-p. 59

McALLISTER, Alexander Mayburn & Delilah Quarles-Aug. 27, 1856, by Hayes Arnold,
Esq.-p. 54

McALLISTER, Geo. & Amanda Wilson-Mar. 8, 1852, by Wm. Burden-p. 40

McBRIDE, ___son E. & Mary Brown-Feb. 23, 1840, by David Snodgrass, Esq.-p. 7

McBRIDE, Charles & Nancy Brown-Sept. 16, 1839, by Sims Dearing, Esq.-p. 6

McBRIDE, Crawford & Mary Mason-Aug. 11, 1845, by Joel Whitley, Esq.-p. 13

McBRIDE, Daniel & Rebecca Davis-July 28, 1839, by John Gillentine, Esq.-p. 5

McBRIDE, Jesse & Mary A. Hathaway-Nov. 7, 1855, by E. W. Denton, Esq.-p. 52

McBRIDE, John J. & Malvina Hodges-Jan. 24, 1850, by Rev. Isaac Denton-p. 33

McBRIDE, John S. & Helen A. Passons-Oct. 23, 1851, by Creed A. Taylor-p. 39

McBRIDE, Spencer & Martha Susannah Nero-Apr. 9, 1854, by Rev. Wm. Burden-p. 48

McBRIDE, Wm. & Becah [Rebecca] Bohannon-Mar. 2, 1837-(L.P.-B.V.)

McBRIDE, Wm. B. & Celia Scoggins-Dec. 25, 1856, by C. A. Taylor, Esq.-p. 54

McBROOM, Anthony & Mary Crook-Aug. 15, 1844, by Shadrick Price, Esq.-p. 18

McCALISS, John E. & Sarah Mitchell-Oct. 6, 1848, by Robt. Hitchcock, Esq.-p. 29

McCANN, James S. & Nancy J. Weaver-Feb. 24, 1847-p. 25

McCARRA, J. F. & Lucinda Womack-July 26, 1849-p. 32

McCONNELL, James A., Sr. & Margaret Harlow-Apr. 23, 1854, by Rev. Wm. Jared-p.48

McCONNELL, Jas. A., Jr. & Matilda Caroline Southard-Oct. 31, 1854, by Rev. Wm. Jared-p. 49

McCORMICK, Christa & Parilee Miller-Dec. 5, 1851, by Wm. C. Johnson-p. 39

McCORMICK, L. D. & Martha Ann Roach-Sept. 16, 1853, by Wm. C. Johnson-p. 46

McCOY, John W. & Matilda Lewis-Aug. 20, 1857, by Wm. Wilson, Esq.-p. 56

McCOY, Jonathan & Rilda Martin-July 13, 1844, by Robt. Hitchcock, Esq.-p. 18

McCULLOUGH, Thos. & Elizabeth Moore-Dec. 26, 1842, by David Snodgrass, Esq.-p.14

McCULLOUGH, Wm. & Tarissa Bussell-Mar. 19, 1854, by Alva Bussell, Esq.-p. 47

McCULLOW, Robt. H. & Eliza Bidwell-Sept. 12, 1839, by David Snodgrass, Esq.-p.6

McCULLOW, Willie R. & Charlotte Bidwell-Nov. 4, 1839, by David Snodgrass, Esq.-p. 6

McDANIEL, Jno. & Judia Manning-Sept. 9, 1845, by Solomon Yeager, Esq.-p. 19

McDANIEL, John & Susan Swindle-July 2, 1857-p. 56

McDANIEL, Wm. & Elizabeth Manning-Oct. 5, 1843, by Wm. Austin, Esq.-p. 16

McDOLE, _____ & Nancy Dildine-Jan. 27, 1839, by Richard Crowder-p. 4

McDONALD, Archibald & Mary Ann Roberts-July 20, 1847-p. 26

McELLIOTT, James & Maria Jane Sherrill-July 9, 1855, by M. C. Dibrell, Esq.-p.50

McELROY, Andrew J. & Jane Webb-Sept. 18, 1845, by Jesse E. Hickman-p. 19

McENTIRE, Thos. & Sarah Lewis-Aug. 22, 1855, by M. C. Dibrell, Esq.-p. 51

McEWIN [See: McQUIN], Elijah & Jariah Bussell-Feb. 19, 1858, by Rev. M. W. McConnell-p. 57

McEWIN, John & Martely Robbins-Nov. 23, 1855, by Rev. L. H. Bennett-p. 52

McGAR, Harmon & Susan Rose-May 26, 1846, by John Swindle, Esq.-p. 23

McGEE, John A. & Caroline Hooper-Jan. 5, 1852, by J. W. Glenn, Esq.-p. 40

McGOWEN, Joseph & Maximilla Short-Nov. 4, 1841, by Rev. Arnold Moss-p. 12

McGOWER, Willie & Tabitha Norris-Dec. 23, 1839, by Rev. Arnold Moss-p. 7

McGUIRE, Gattiff & Mary Taylor-Jan. 23, 1844, by Robt. H. McManus-p. 17

McGUIRE, Jesse & Martha Scurlock-Sept. 10, 1856-p. 54

McGUIRE, Thos. J. & Phila Ann Berry-Feb. 17, 1857, by D. M. Southard, Esq.-p.55

McGUIRE, Wm. & Mary Davis-Dec. 18, 1838, by John Gillentine, Esq.-p. 4

MACKEY, John & Nancy Chisum-Dec. 20, 1838, by Wm. C. Bounds, Esq.-p. 4

MACKIE, Robt. & Sarah Sailors-Feb. 17, 1847, by Rev. John B. Poniter-p. 25

McKINNEY, Emanuel G. & Manerva Long-Mar. 7, 1840, by David Snodgrass, Esq.-p. 8

McKINNEY, Thos. J.B. & Meekey Ann Jarvis-Dec. 20, 1855, by Wm. M. Anderson, Esq.-p. 52

McMANUS, Samuel V. & Mary Jane Brown-Mar. 2, 1858-p. 57

McMILLAN, James C. & Sarah Bryan-Oct. 30, 1850-p. 36

McNABB, Andrew J. & Mariah Farris-Jan. 4, 1848-p. 27

McNEELY, John & Rachel Glenn-_____ __, 1841-p. 10

McNEIL, Wm. W. & Martha Dunn-Sept. 12, 1850-p. 35

McQUIN [McEWIN], James M. & Harriet L. Watson-Mar. 8, 1847-p. 25

MADEWELL, David M. & Nancy M.A.E. Graham-Aug. 17, 1848, by Rev. D.H. Morgan-p.29

MADEWELL, Jas. & Polly Dixon-Apr. 14, 1817-(L.P.-B.V.)

MADEWELL, John & Judith Grant-Jan. 23, 1841, by Wm. Hudgens, Esq.-p. 11

MADEWELL, Jno. R. & Sarah Phillips-Dec. 11, 1838, by Isaac Buck, Esq.-p. 4

MADISON, Russell D. & Salila Crain-June 27, 1857-p. 56

MADISON, Wesley & Eliza Jane Ross-May 15, 1858, by Rev. James Herd-p. 58

MAIDWELL, Thos. & Pernella Clash-Dec. 11, 1846-p. 24

MALLOY, James & Frances M. Shaw-Jan. 26, 1851, by R. R. Richey-p. 36

MANES, Bartholomew & Elizabeth McCullough-Oct. 4, 1855, by Alva Bussell, Esq.-p. 51

MANN, John Henry & Sarah Scoggin-circa 1830-[Ref: THE NASHVILLE NEWS (Nashville, Ark.), Sept. 3, 1893-(Obituary Notice). She was dau. of Rev. John & Elizabeth (White) Scoggin, Jr. He was a Methodist Circuit-Rider minister.]

MANNING, Henry E. & Susan A. Miller-Sept. 5, 1850, by Creed A. Taylor, Esq.-p.35

MANNING, Pleasant F. & Heilen Vaugn-Jan. 8, 1846, by Wm. Austin, Esq.-p. 21

MANOR, Vincen & Laniza Hill-Mar. 29, 1849-p. 31

MANOR, Wamon L. & Amanda Doyle-Oct. 3, 1849, by Rev. M. Y. Brockett-p. 32

MANUS, John P. & Malinda C. Hitchcock-Oct. 9, 1856, by Alvey Bussell, Esq.-p.54 [Is this a double wedding? See: Wm. H. Bennett.]

MARCHBANKS, Jasper & Margaret J. Irwin-Apr. 30, 1846, by Wm. Glenn, Esq.-p. 23

MARCHBANKS, Jonathan & Margaret Buck-Jan. 20, 1842, by Rev. Stephen B. Lyles-p.13

MARKHAM, Lewis & Sarah Norris-May 9, 1845-p. 19

MARKHAM, Westley & Birdy Hearn-July 12, 1838, by Rev. Arnold Moss-p. 2

MARKUM, Jasper & Polly Clark-Dec. 23, 1845, by Rev. Peter Burum-p. 21

MARLOW, John & Nancy (?)McMath-May 13, 1855, by Rev. Thos. E. Hutson-p. 50

MARLOW, Wm. & Elizabeth Ann Blankenship-Jan. 5, 1854, by Elijah W. Denton-p. 47

MARREMAN, Smith & Allisaria J. Franks-May 31, 1846, by Joél Whitley, Esq.-p. 23

MARSH, Jehoida & Angeletta Kidwell-Dec. 19, 1850, by D. Snodgrass, Esq.-p. 36

MARTIN, David & Nancy Cole-Nov. 15, 1819-(L.P.-B.V.)

MARTIN, David H. & Amanda Denton-Feb. 8, 1856, by J. A. Knowles, Esq.-p. 52

MARTIN, John & Sarah Hutson-Aug. 2, 1853, by Rev. Jeremiah Webb-p. 45

MARTIN, Mordecai & Nancy Ann Farley-Sept. 20, 1855, by Alvey Bussell, Esq.-p.51

MARTIN, Robert & Elizabeth Herd-Aug. 8, 1838-p. 2

MARTIN, Sam'l. H. & Rebecca Bryant-Nov. 2, 1839, by Rev. Levi Perkins-p. 6

MARTIN, Wm. H. & Frances Eller-May 2, 1858, by David Snodgrass, Esq.-p. 58

MASON, George & Margaret Kerby-Aug. 22, 1853-p. 45

MASON, Jesse & Jane (?)Millyette-June 6, 1839-p. 5

MASON, John & Mahala Bryan-Nov. 9, 1854, by Wm. Wilson, Esq.-p. 49

MASON, Phillip & Nancy Butram-Oct. 11, 1854, by Rich. Bradley, Esq.-p. 49

MASSA, Adam & Jane Thomas-Feb. 1, 1846(?)-[between June 4 & 7, 1840]-by Alvey Bussell, Esq.-p. 9

MASSA, John & Susannah Duncan-Feb. 3, 1853, by Jas. B. Lowrey, Esq.-p. 44

MASSA, Thos. & Clarissa Henry-June 23, 1851, by Creed A. Taylor, Esq.-p. 38

MASSA, Wm. & Sarah Thomas-Dec. 7, 1851-p. 39

MATLOCK, Elcana D. & Diana Lyda-Aug. 31, 1842, by Wm. Glenn, Esq.-p. 13

MATLOCK, Harrison & Lucinda Walker-Nov. 1, 1854, by J. W. Merslom, Esq.-p. 49

MATLOCK, Wm. & Susan Manefee-June 7, 1845, by Jos. G. Mitchell, Esq.-p. 19

MAULDIN, Richard & Anna Turner-Aug. 17, 1842, by R. H. McManus, Esq.-p. 13

MAULDIN, Tucker & Hannah Duncan-June 19, 1844-p. 18

MAYNARD, Levi & Rebecca Whitaker-May 5, 1851, by John Madewell, Esq.-p. 38

MAYNOR, Vincent & Elizabeth Henderson-Feb. 22, 1851, by Rev. R. R. Richey-p. 37

MAYNOR, William & Sarah Whitaker-Jan. 29, 1851, by John Madewell, Esq.-p. 37

MAYSE, Benjamin & Rebecca Anderson-Feb. 24, 1851-p. 37

MEDLEY, James & Matilda Pain-Jan. 5, 1853, by Wm. Clayton, Esq.-p. 43

MEDLEY, Mark & Elizabeth Dunn-Feb. 5, 1843, by Wm. R. Tucker, Esq.-p. 15

MEEKER, Edwin H. & Emaline J. Worley-Nov. 7, 1842-p. 14

MERCER, Nicholas & Jane Lincoln-Sept. 10, 1848, by Rev. Wm. Jared-p. 29

MEREDITH, James W. & Mary L. Lisk-May 13, 1858, by Rev. M. Y. Brockett-p. 58

MEREDITH, Joseph B. & Margaret E. Carrick-Dec. 22, 1852, by Wm. Jarred-p. 43

METCALF, Charles W. & Evaline Simpson-May 10, 1848, by Rev. E. A. Smith-p. 28

METCALF, Thos. & Susan Potts-Feb. 13, 1840, by Sims Dearing, Esq.-p. 7

METCALF, Thos. C. & Liza Ann Yeager-Dec. 21, 1840-p. 10

METCALF, Wm. & Elizabeth Cameron-Jan. 15, 1850, by Rev. J. E. Hickman-p. 33

METCALF, Wm. C. & Sarah M. Bowman-June 23, 1841, by Robt. H. McMann, Esq.-p. 11

METKIFF, Thos. C. & Miss Ann J. Pass-Jan. 25, 1841-p. 10

[See also, MITKIFF]

MILLER, Donald & Creacy [Lucretia] Hutson-Jan. 17, 1812, Geo. Hutson, Bondsman-(L.P.-B.V)

MILLER, George W. & Susannah Roberts-Oct. 28, 1858, by Rev. H. B. Johnson-p. 59

MILLER, John, Jr. & Frances Miller-Sept. 24, 1850, by J. H. Graham, Esq.-p. 35

MILLER, John H. & Clementine Lewis-Dec. 16, 1851-p. 39

MILLER, Luin & Margaret C. Officer-Nov. 9, 1840-p. 9

MILLER, Robert & Susan F. Couch-Feb. 5, 1846, by Rev. James Herd-p. 22

MILLER, Samuel, Jr. & Franky Frasur-Apr. 25, 1844-p. 17

MILLER, Wm. H. & Mary Lewis-Oct. 4, 1857, by John W. Mitchell, Esq.-p. 56

MILLER, Wm. W. & Elizabeth Wood-Nov. 22, 1838, by Rev. Ozias Denton-p. 3

MILLER, Willson S. & Tabitha B. Phillips-Nov. 20, 1839, by Rev. Abel Hutson-p. 6

MILLS, Hezekiah & Emaline Miller-Sept. 13, 1852-p. 42

MILLS, Hezekiah & Mrs. Agnes Frasier-Sept. 25, 1856, by John Willhite, Esq.-p.54

MILLS, John W. & Martha Ann Walker-Sept. 16, 1857, by Alvey Bussell, Esq.-p. 54

MILLS, Lewis & Nancy J. Bradford-Apr. 27, 1848, by Rev. Thos. Stone-p. 28

MILLSAP, Thos. & Mary J. Wilhite-Nov. 20, 1846, by Wm. Glenn, Esq.-p. 24

MILLSAPS, Perry & Martha Hamilton-Sept. 15, 1849-p. 32

MITCHELL, A. A. & Mary C. Newman-Oct. 15, 1849-p. 32

MITCHELL, Charter W. & Susan Ditty-Feb. 16, 1847-p. 25

MITCHELL, James C. & Mary Hill-Nov. 1, 1855, by Rev. M. Y. Brockett-p. 52

MITCHELL, Jesse & Frances Jane Smith-June 18, 1850, by Wm. Clayton, Esq.-p. 34

MITCHELL, John A. & Elizabeth Collier-Dec. 20, 1841-(not returned)-p. 12

MITCHELL, Joseph G. & Teresa Shaw-Feb. 10, 1852, by Rev. M. Y. Brockett-p. 40

MITCHELL, Spencer & Nancy Wilson-Dec. 18, 1842, by Anderson S. Rogers, Esq.-p.14

MITCHELL, Wm. H. & Jane Smith-Aug. 24, 1848, by Rev. Levi Perkins-p. 29

MITCHELL, Wm. I. & Amanda Deweese-Jan. 19, 1854, by Rev. Wm. Jared-p. 47

MITCHELL, Wm. L. & Elizabeth Warren-Apr. 27, 1852, by Rev. J. E. Hickman-p. 41

MITKIFF, Thos. (?)S. & Sarah Thomas-May 14, 1847-p. 25

MITKIFF, Wm. C. & Permelia Billingsly-Aug. 31, 1847-p. 26. [Descendants say her
name was Camelia.]

MONTGOMERY, John H. & Elizabeth Hickey-Dec. 23, 1841-(not returned)-p. 12

MONTGOMERY, Leftwich & Charlotte Massa-Oct. 26, 1846-p. 24

MONTGOMERY, Simpson & Susan Felts-June 17, 1848, by Robt. Hitchcock-p. 29

MONNEYHAM, Wm. & Lucinda McCluin-June 18, 1839, by Tilman Brown-p. 5

MOON [See: MOORE]

MOONEYHAM, Jesse & Mary Davis-Mar. 1, 1844-p. 17

MOORE, Calvin & Jane Edmonds-Mar. 23, 1858, by Hayse Arnold, Esq.-p. 57

MOORE, Christopher & Susan Keathly-Mar. 5, 1856, by E. W. Denton, Esq.-p. 53

MOORE, Hugh L. C. & Lee Ann Greer-Aug. 5, 1852, by Rev. James Herd-p. 42

MOORE, James & Lee Ann Farley-Dec. 28, 1850-p. 36

MOORE [MOON], Jonathan H. & Miss Margarett P. Huddleston-May 13, 1845-p. 19

MOORE, Joseph & Jistin Baker-May 21, 1843, by Anderson S. Rogers, Esq.-p. 15

MOORE, Joseph & Martha Mitchell-Dec. 21, 1858, by Rev. Jas. Herd-p. 59

MOORE, Wm. M. & Agness Stewart-Dec. 29, 1842, by David Snodgrass, Esq.-p. 14

MOORE, Wm. M. & Marion Meek-Mar. 17, 1858-p. 57

MOORE, William N. & Louisa Broyles-Sept. 11, 1842, by Richd. Bradley, Esq.-p.14

MOORE, Wm. N. & Mahala Bohanon-May 26, 1847-p. 26

MORRIS, Benjamin & Sally Nemore-June 14, 1838, by Rev. Corder Stone-p. 2

MORRIS, Wm. & Dorcas Steel-June 28, 1850, by Robt. Hitchcock, Esq.-p. 35

MOSELY, Charles & Sarah S. Anderson-Nov. 18, 1850-p. 36

MOSLEY, Wm. B. & Mary Ann Creson-Mar. 23, 1844, by Jno. Pennington, Esq.-p. 17

MOSS, Arnold & Prissee [Priscilla] Holland-Dec. 30, 1845, by Rev. Arnold Moss-p. 21

MOSS, Ebenezer & Rebecca Holland-Sept. 7, 1848, by John L. Grissom, Esq.-p. 29

MOSS, James Monroe & Rhoda Short-Sept. 7, 1848, by Rev. James Herd-p. 29

MOSS, Obediah & Elizabeth J. Bryan-Nov. 2, 1848, by Wm. W. Moore, Esq.-p. 30

MURPHEE, Levi & Keziah Martha Watson-June 12, 1840-p. 9

MURPHEY, Wm. & Sarah Jones-Aug. 23, 1849, by Wm. Clayton, Esq.-p. 32

MURPHY, John J. & Ann Vass-Nov. 2, 1854, by Rev. Wm. Jared-p. 49

MURRAY, Edward & Martha White-Feb. 27, 1840, by Rev. John A. Jones-p. 8. [She was dau. of Woodson Phillips & Nancy (Mitchell) White.]

MURRAY, Thos. B. & Mary Goodbar-Nov. 30, 1852, by Rev. J. H. Richey-p. 43

MYATT, Alexander & Elizabeth Cardwell-Sept. 10, 1841-(not returned)-p. 12

MYATT, Alfred & Nancy Cardwell-Mar. 2, 1841, by Rev. Levi Perkins-p. 10

NARRAMORE, Andrew & Mary Johnston-Aug. 16, 1845, by Thos. Jones, Esq.-p. 19

NASH, James & Alsy Gentry-Apr. 15, 1848, by Robt. Hitchcock, Esq.-p. 28

NASH, Newton & America Lafevers-Oct. 19, 1857, by Alvey Bussell, Esq.-p. 56

NASH, Wm. & Elizabeth Felts-July 6, 1842, by Shadrach Price, Esq.-p.13

NELSON, Jacob & Susannah Pinegar-Oct. 30, 1824-(L.P.-B.V.)

NELSON, James H. & Amey J. Grime-Apr. 20, 1854, by Rev. Nathan Judd-p. 48

NELSON Wm. E. & Mary Ann Snodgrass-Feb. 26, 1846, by Rev. Jesse E. Hickman-p.22

NETHERTON, Wm. & Rebecca Morrison-Mar. 5, 1839, by D. Snodgrass, Esq.-p. 4

NEWMAN, Michael H. & Mary Jane Scott-Nov. 25, 1858, by Richard Bradley, Esq.-p.59

NICHOLAS, James O. & Jane E. Gillialand-Mar. 23, 1841, by Rev. Jesse E. Hickman-p. 11

NICHOLAS, Jonathan & Nancy Griffith-July 17, 1845, by John Pennington, Esq.-p.21

NICHOLAS, Lincoln & Mary Bohannon-July 17, 1845, by Rev. Jesse E. Hickman-p. 19

NICHOLAS, Thos. T. & Ariselar Moon-Oct. 5, 1846-p. 23

NICHOLS, _____ & Elizabeth Bohannon-July 24, 1838, by John Bryan, Esq.-p. 2

NICKELS, _____ & Mary Harlow-Dec. 6, 1838, by Rev. Ozias Denton-p. 3

NOAKS, Elias B. & Lucy A. W. Colley-Mar. 18, 1840, by Wm. Little, Esq.-p. 8

NORRIS, Avery & Martha Hutson-Dec. 20, 1855, by Rev. Thos. E. Hutson-p. 52

NORRIS, Isham & Sarah Jane Maynor-June 30, 1852, by Levi Jarvis, Esq.-p. 41

NORRIS, Silas & Eliza Walling-Sept. 26, 1846, by Joseph Gist, Esq.-p. 23

NORRIS, Wm. R. & Nancy Bohannon-June 7, 1849, by Jesse B. Clark, Esq.-p. 32

OAKS, Alexander & Margaret Elvira Graham-Apr. 28, 1853, by Wm. Burden, M.G.-p.44

OFFICER, Alexander J. & Lucinda Bohannon-Nov. 7, 1844, by Rev. Thos. Stone-p. 18

OFFICER, James & Leann Glenn-Sept. 30, 1839, by David Snodgrass, Esq.-p. 6

OFFICER, Wm. & Emily Snodgrass-Apr. 25, 1858, by M. C. Dibrell-p. 57

OGDEN, George & Easther Smith-Sept. 8, 1839, by Rev. Andrew McBride-p. 6

OGDEN, George W. & Sarah Lance-Nov. 17, 1858, by M. C. Dibrell, Esq.-p. 59

OVERBY, Wm. & Lucinda Rogers-Mar. 9, 1843, by Robt. H. McManus, Esq.-p. 15

OWENS, Greenberry & Margaret E. Robbins-Jan. 6, 1853, by Rev. ___ James-p. 43

OWENS, Jacob & Rebecca Moore-July 27, 1839-p. 5

PACE, Joseph & Rachel Ross-Mar. 25, 1856, by James A. Knowles, Esq.-p. 53

PACK, Joseph & Martha Snider-Apr. 17, 1845-p. 19

PARKER, Joseph A. & Selicia E. Clark-Oct. 11, 1857, by James A. Knowles, Esq.-p. 56

PARKER, W. H. & Angeletty Mercer-Jan. 31, 1849, by Wm. W. Moore, Esq.-p. 31

PARKER, Wilson & Mary Moore-Sept. 19, 1839, by David Snodgrass, Esq.-p. 6

PARMER, Jefferson & Nancy Mason-Feb. 15, 1843, by Rev. Corder Stone-p. 15

PARRISH, John & Nancy T. _____-Aug. 17, 1838, by Wm. C. Bounds-p. 2

PARSONS, Francis & Mary Jane Boyd-Aug. 19, 1852, by Rev. Wm. Burden-p. 42

PARSONS, John & Nora [Lona] Flinn-May 7, 1826, by Andrew Townsend, J.P.-(L.P.-B.V.)

PARSONS, John & Hila Baker-Mar. 2, 1854, by John Crook, Esq.-p. 47

PASKELL, Wm. & Margaret Sayers-June 28, 1838, by Richard Crowder, Esq.-p. 2

PASS, Lafatte & Camelian Yeager-Apr. 7, 1846, by Solomon Yeager, Esq.-p. 22

PASS, N. F. & Indianna Farley-Dec. 9, 1847, by Solomon Yeager, Esq.-p. 27

PATTERSON, L. G. & Margaret Amanda Stewart-Apr. 12, 1849, by Rev. Wm. Jared-p. 31

PATTON, Joseph & Jane Roach-Oct. 5, 1848-p. 30

PATTON, Josiah & Elenor Moore-Oct. 6, 1839, by Elijah Frost, Esq.-p. 6

PATTON, Robt. & Susan Jane Rogers-Nov. 21, 1857, by M. C. Dibrell, Esq.-p. 56

PAYNE, Alexander & Rosanna Millsap-Oct. 15, 1855, by Rev. Leonidas H. Bennett-p.51

PEAK, James K. & Luraney Bounds-Oct. 15, 1850, by Rev. Thos. Stone-p. 35

PEARON, John & Trimanda M.C. Ketcherside-July 19, 1855, by Rev. M.Y. Brockett-p.51

PEARSON, Usrey & Margaret White-Nov. 9, 1838, by Wm. Little, Esq.-p. 3

PENDERGRASS, John E. & Martha Gregory-Feb. 18, 1849, by Rev. Ozias Denton-p. 31

PENNINGTON, Dabner & Margaret Bradford-Dec. 15, 1840, by Wm. C. Bounds, Esq.-p.10

PENNINGTON, Emory & Eliza Cash-Sept. 16, 1839, by Rev. Corder Stone-p. 6

PENNINGTON, Emory & Miss Juliann Henry-Jan. 29, 1845-p. 19

PENNINGTON, Joshua, Jr. & Eliza Couch-Apr. 6, 1843, by Wm. Austin, Esq.-p. 15

PENNINGTON, Silles & Elizabeth Bradford-Aug. 20, 1846, by Rev. Thos. Stone-p. 24

PERKINS, Wm. J. & Elizabeth J. Mills-Aug. 18, 1842, by Rev. Levi Perkins-p. 13

PERRY, Solomon A. & Nancy Fisher-Nov. 29, 1849-p. 33

PETILLO, James F. & Elizabeth Lollar-Sept. 18, 1851, by Robt. Hitchcock, Esq.-p. 39

PHIFER, James & Jane Goddard-Dec. 8, 1842, by Wm. Austin, Esq.-p. 14

PHILLIPS, Andrew & Delila Waddle-Oct. 17, 1846, by Joel Whitley, Esq.-p. 24

PHILLIPS, Levi & Ellinor Ellison-June 5, 1845, by John Pennington, Esq.-p. 21

PHILLIPS, Washington & Hannah Harris-May 17, 1856, by Hayes Arnold, Esq.-p. 53

PHY, Daniel & Martha Dickerson-June 8, 1848, by W. K. Bradford-p. 28

PHY, Daniel & Elizabeth Bradford-Dec. 18, 1850-p. 36

PIPPIN, Amos & Lydia Barnes-Apr. 28, 1853, by Thos. Stone, M.G.-p. 44

PIRTLE, Foster A. & Margaret Winstead-Nov. 26, 1851-p. 39

PIRTLE, Geo. W., Jr. & Lucinda Pirtle-Dec. 31, 1839, by Rev. S. G. Buxton-p. 7

PIRTLE, Perry W. & Emily S. A. Pollard-Dec. 2, 1852-p. 43

POLLARD, E_____ M. R. & Amanda M. Arnold-Aug. 28, 1856-p. 54

POLLARD, George W. & Lydia M. Dotson-June 9, 1847-p. 26

POLLARD, Joshua & Sarah Wilson-Sept. 11, 1858-p. 58

POLLARD, Luce & Sarah Jordon-June 18, 1856-p. 53

POLLARD, Wm. & Christiana J. Mayse-Apr. 21, 1850, by J. L. Grissom, Esq.-p. 34

POPE, Thos. & Martha Snodgrass-Mar. 27, 1851, by Rev. Jesse E. Hickman-p. 37

POTEET, James & Sarah Savage-Feb. 27, 1839-p. 4

POTEET, Thomas J. & Amanda Barnes-Oct. 31, 1848, by Joseph D. Hyder, Esq.-p. 30

POTEET, Thos. J. & Jane Carland-Nov. 28, 1849, by Robert Hitchcock, Esq.-p. 33

POTTS, Andrew L. & Elsy England-Mar. 22, 1841-(Issued-not returned)-p. 11

POTTS, Patrick & Bethiah Beshears-May 4, 1848, by Robt. Hitchcock, Esq.-p. 28

POTTS, Wm. & Ruth B. Tucker-Nov. 25, 1850-p. 36

POWELL, Balew & Frances Parish-Feb. 26, 1850-p. 34

POWELL, J. C. & Jane A. Dodson-Mar. 5, 1857, by M. G. Dibrell, Esq.-p. 55

POWELL, Wm. & Harriet Farris-Oct. 20, 1847-p. 27

PRATER, Josiah, Jr. & Nancy Kirby-Oct. 29, 1858, by John J. Duncan, Esq.-p. 59

PRATER, Moses & Malinda Dodson-Feb. 21, 1849, by Rev. John Green-p. 31

PRATT, James M. & Nancy J. Upchurch-June 14, 1843, by Rev. I. C. Woodward-p. 15

PRICE, Andres & Parmetas Buyers-July 18, 1846-p. 23

PRICE, Andrew & Parmetus Byers-Apr. 3, 1842, by Wm. Little, Esq.-p. 13

PRICE, Henry F. & Rebecca M. Chilcutt-May 9, 1854, by Rev. Wm. Jared-p. 48

PRICE, Llewellyn & Jane Malden-Apr. 16, 1840, by Geo. Defrees, Esq.-p. 8

PRICE, Lore[n]zo D. & Mary Stewart-Sept. 26, 1858, by Alexr. Oliver, Esq.-p. 58

PRICE, Merrion & Susannah Lee-May 4, 1853, by Rev. Wm. Goodwin-p. 44

PRICE, Thomas & Rosa Wetherford-Feb. 18, 1844, by Jno. Wilhite, Esq.-p. 17

PRINCE, Wm. & Eliza Ann Phy-Nov. 29, 1847, by John Wilhite, Esq.-p. 27

PRINCE, Wm. & Sally Ann Sparkman-Oct. 6, 1847-p. 27

PROCK, Jahew H. & Louisa Stinett-Feb. 17, 1858, by John J. Duncan, Esq.-p. 57

PROCK, Wm. Riley & Hester Ann Lowell-Feb. 15, 1855, by Rev. Wm. Burden-p. 50

PROVINCE, Andrew & Eliza J. Slatten-June 26, 1841-(not returned)-p. 11

PROVINCE, Hiram & Rachel Markum-July 28, 1842 ("Soon after".), by Rev. Peter
        Burem, Esq.-p. 13

PUCKETT, John & Rhody Lyda-Dec. 4, 1809-(L.P.-B.V.)-[Oldest existing record.]

PURSER, Joshua & Sntha Short-Mar. 7, 1843, by Rev. Arnold Moss-p. 15

QUARLES, John & Jamima Morgan-Mar. 25, 1850-p. 34

QUILLEN, John & Nancy Ann Jane Robbins-Oct. 10, 1852, by Wm. I. Russell, Esq.-p.42

RAMSEY, Austin & Margrett Holeman-Dec. 9, 1847, by John Wilhite, Esq.-p. 27

RAMSEY, Blackman A. & Eliza Jett-Feb. 19, 1840, by Rev. John H[enry] Mann-p. 7

RAMSEY, Jesse & Martha J. James-July 25, 1858, by John W. Mitchell, Esq.-p. 58

RAMSEY, Thomas & Susannah Holman-Aug. 28, 1853, by D. L. Snodgrass, Esq.-p. 45

RAMSEY, William & Margaret Ramsey-July 13, 1853, by Rev. Thos. Stone-p. 45

RANDOLPH, Bartlett & Nancy Patton-July 13, 1845, by John Pennington, Esq.-p. 22

RANDOLPH, Chisom, Jr. & Polly Ann Patrick-Apr. 18, 1851, by Wm. C. Johnson, Esq.-p. 37

RANDOLPH, Dudley & Susan D. Hill-Dec. 7, 1849-p. 33

RANDOLPH, Isaac & Judde Cooper-Nov. 6, 1844, by Richd. Bradley, Esq.-p. 18

RANDOLPH, John W. & Lucy Ann Cooper-Aug. 5, 1853, by Wm. C. Johnson-p. 45

RANDOLPH, Joseph & Polly Daniel-Aug. 7, 1845, by Rev. Thos. Stone-p. 22

RANDOLPH, Peyton & Mary Cooper-Aug. 15, 1840, by Sims Dearing, Esq.-p. 9. [She was dau. of Alexander, a Revol. soldier.]

RANDOLPH, Pleasant & Margeagett Jackson-Oct. 30, 1846-p. 24

RANDOLPH, Preston & Manerva Randolph-Aug. 14, 1848, by Solomon Yeager, Esq.-p.29

RANNEY, Wm. & Melinda Beshears-Apr. 25, 1846, by Robt. Hitchcock, Esq.-p. 23

RAY, Daniel M. & Mary Ditty-Sept. 26, 1844, by Rev. Jesse Hickman-p. 18

RAY, Joshua H. & Elizabeth Ditty-Oct. 11, 1849, by Rev. Wm. Jared-p. 32

REAGAN, James J. & Evaline Anderson-Dec. 27, 1855, by Elijah W. Denton, Esq.-p.52

REAL, E. B. F. & Elizabeth Greer-Dec. 23, 1847, by Isaac Denton, M.G.-p. 27

REAL, Geo. W. & Martha J. Hill-Oct. 18, 1855, by Rev. Jas. H. Morgan-p. 51

REDAFORD, Larkin & Lila Worley-Mar. 2, 1849-p. 31

REEVES, James W. & Sarah Moss-June 8, 1849-p. 32

REYNOLD, John B. & Sarah Cloyd-Oct. 8, 1848, by Shadrick Price, Esq.-p. 30

REYNOLDS, Wm. & Rhody P. Frost-Dec. 22, 1853, by John Crook, Esq.-p. 46

RHEA, Bird S. & Ann E. Taylor-Aug. 24, 1845, by Elijah W. Denton, Esq.-p. 19

RHEA, James W. & Mary M. Mills-Dec. 1, 1842, by Rev. Levi Perkins-p. 14

RHEA, John S. & Amanda J. England-Dec. 23, 1857, by Rev. James K. Lansden-p. 57

RICE, Jesse G. & Josephine Plummer-Jan. 24, 1856, by Rev. Elias King-p. 52

RICE, John & Marinda Caroline Massa-Nov. 11, 1855, by Rev. J. J. James-p. 51

RICE, Theodorick B. & Polly Herbert-Mar. 28, 1816-(L.P.-B.V.)

RICE, Wm. & Mary Massa-Mar. 7, 1839-p. 4

RICHARDS, Daniel R. & Mary Jane Taylor-Apr. 3, 1855, by Rev. A. Deitz-p. 50

RICHARDS, Henderson K. & Mary Graham-July 31, 1839-p. 5

RICHARDS, Isham & Priscilla D. Gillentine-Oct. 23, 1843, by Rev. Jas. H. Morgan-p. 16

RICHARDSON, Andrew J. & Frances E. J. Weaver-July 18, 1857-p. 56

RICHARDSON, Jno. & Jude Bean-Aug. 17, 1845, by Rev. Ozias Denton-p. 19

RICHEY, James H. & Elizabeth Snodgrass-Feb. 7, 1854, by Rev. A. F. Lawrence-p.47

RICKMAN, Nicholas & Lucinda Roberts-Jan. 6, 1848, by M. C. Dibrell, Esq.-p. 27

RIDDLES, John W. & Rhoda Flinn-Nov. 24, 1847-p. 27

RIGSBY, Canady & Vina Manos-Dec. 14, 1841, by James Knowles-p. 12

RIGSBY, John & Margrett Adams-Nov. 4, 1845, by John Pennington, Esq.-p. 22

RIGSBY, Milton & Mary Ann Clouse-Dec. 14, 1849, by Wm. P. Russell, Esq.-p. 33

RIGSBY, Russell & Sarah Hutchings-Oct. 12, 1838, by Jas. T. Hayes, Esq.-p. 3

ROBBINS, Lewis & Sarah Herd-May 30, 1857, by W. E. Camp, Esq.-p. 55

ROBBINS, Wm. & Susan Cope-Oct. 10, 1850, by Rev. James Herd-p. 35

ROBBINS, Wm. Houston & Marteela Anderson-Jan. 2, 1851, by Rev. R. R. Richey-p.36

ROBERSON, Charles & Sarah Jackson-Apr. 16, 1850, by John Madewell, Esq.-p. 34

ROBERSON, James J. & Nancy Smith-July 25, 1855, by John Crook, Esq.-p. 51

ROBERSON, John & Lucy Henry-Apr. 8, 1851, by Rev. Thos. Stone-p. 37

ROBERSON, Levi & Manerva Blankenship-Oct. 10, 1852, by W. L. Woods, Esq.-p. 42

ROBERTS, Caswell C. & Stacy Simmons-Dec. 10, 1842, by Thos. Green, Esq.-p. 14

ROBERTS, Ellis H. & Diana Swindle-Sept. 20, 1839, by Rev. S. G. Buxton-p. 6

ROBERTS, Francis A. & Elizabeth Denton-July 13, 1848, by Rev. Thos. E. Hutson-p. 29

ROBERTS, Francis A. & Martha Ann Denton-Apr. 16, 1855, by W. Webb, Esq.-p. 50

ROBERTS, James M. & Melrainy Holland-Dec. 23, 1851, by Rev. T. E. Hutson-p. 40

ROBERTS, Jesse & Sarah Lay-Nov. 26, 1844, by Rev. Isaac Denton-p. 18

ROBERTS, Jesse & Elizabeth Yeats-Oct. 28, 1851, by Rev. T. E. Hutson-p. 39

ROBERTS, Jesse & Winney Brown-Dec. 2, 1852-p. 43

ROBERTS, John & Mary Ann Ramsey-Feb. 25, 1847, by John Wilhite, Esq.-p. 25

ROBERTS, John A. & Louisa D. Harris-Jan. 15, 1850, by Robt. Hitchcock, Esq.-p.33

ROBERTS, John A. & Sarah Bogarth-Oct. 13, 1850, by Rev. Isaac Denton-p. 35

ROBERTS, John W. & Jane Rickman-Oct. 22, 1846-p. 24

ROBERTS, John W. & Edith Earles-Sept. 15, 1855, by Patrick Moore, M.G.-p. 51

ROBERTS, Joseph & Mary Jane Rogers-Oct. 12, 1852, by Rev. M. W. McConnell-p. 42

ROBERTS, Joseph W. & Sarah Underwood-June 30, 1839[38?], by Jesse Walling, Esq.-p. 3

ROBERTS, Robt. & Cynthiann Henry-Aug. 28, 1839, by Isaac Buck-p. 5

ROBERTS, Robt. & Mahaly Conly-Oct. 17, 1858, by Rich. Bradley, Esq.-p. 58

ROBERTS, Thomas & Isabel Swindle-Apr. 7, 1841, by Rev. Abel Hutson-p. 11

ROBERTS, Wm. C. & Mahala Copeland-Jan. 9, 1853, by Rev. T. E. Hutson-p. 43

ROBERTSON, Pleasant & Jane Bohannon-Aug. 28, 1841-(not returned)-p. 12

ROBERTSON, Wm. & Phebe Roberts-Oct. 11, 1843, by John Smith, Esq.-p. 16

ROBERTSON, Wm. & Sarah Tucker-Sept. 15, 1853, by Levi Jarvis, Esq.-p. 45

ROBINSON, Alexander C. & Malissa Moore-Jan. 15, 1848-p. 27

ROBINSON, Eli & Temperance Lewis-Feb. 22, 1846, by Rev. Ozias Denton-p. 22

ROBINSON, Geo. W. P. & Mary Jane Womack-Nov. 9, 1850-p. 36

ROBINSON, James & Mary Ann McCormick-Jan. 19, 1848-p. 27

ROBINSON, James M. & Rebecca England-Oct. 22, 1851, by Andrew Graham-p. 39

ROBINSON, John H. & Sally Simpson-Nov. 21, 1839-p. 7

ROBINSON, Manuel & Lucinda Cash-Sept. 22, 1838, by Elisha Cameron, Esq.-p. 3

ROBISON, John & Senora J. Wilhite-Aug. 11, 1856, by Richard Simpson, Esq.-p. 54

ROBISON, Lawson & Wincy Broyles-July 22, 1838, by Elisha Cameron, Esq.-p. 2

RODGERS, David G. & Sarah Glover-Oct. 6, 1847-p. 27

RODGERS, Henry & Elizabeth Stanley-Feb. 28, 1844, by Robt. H. McManus, Esq.-p.17

ROGERS, George & Isabella Mitchell-Jan. 27, 1852, by Wm. Clayton, Esq.-p. 40

ROGERS, James & Nancy Dukes-Jan. 9, 1842, by Anderson S. Rogers, Esq.-p. 12

ROGERS, James M. & Mary R. Mitchell-Apr. 22, 1852, by Wm. Clayton, Esq.-p. 41

ROGERS, John M. & Elizabeth M. Rogers-Nov. 5, 1841, by Wm. R. Tucker, Esq.-p. 12

ROGERS, Joseph M. & Polleymena Jones-Feb. 5, 1846, by Joel Whitley, Esq.-p. 22

ROGERS, Thomas G. & Elizabeth Overbee-Jan. 27, 1842, by Robt. H. McManus, Esq.-p. 13

ROGERS, William & Jane Gracy-Mar. 15, 1848, by Jos. G. Mitchell, Esq.-p. 28

ROGERS, Wm. D. & Mary Roberts-May 23, 1855, by D. M. Southard, Esq.-p. 50

ROLLINS, Thos. & Catherine Hopkins-Sept. 20, 1838, by John Gillentine-p. 3

ROSE, Leroy B. & Eliza Jones-Sept. 14, 1852, by Wm. Clayton, Esq.-p. 42

RUNNELLS, John & Ellen Copeland-Dec. 18, 1846-p. 24

RUSSELL, E. Jefferson & Fanny Price-Aug. 7, 1850, by Shade Price, Esq.-p. 35

RUSSELL, Joseph H. & Mary Walling-Sept. 22, 1839, by Jesse Walling-p. 6

RUSSELL, Waman M. & Nancy Y. Gracy-Feb. 18, 1858, by Rev. M. Y. Brockett-p. 57

RUSSELL, Wm. D. & Mary R. Holland-Feb. 1, 1854, by Levi Jarvis-p. 47

RUSSELL, Wm. M. & Susan Bryan-Jan. 8, 1852, by M. Y. Brockett-p. 40

RUTLEDGE, Charles & Minerva Moore-Nov. 30, 1843, by Thos. Cooper, Esq.-p. 16

SABIN, Lyman & Nancy Berry-Mar. 14, 1839, by Asa Certain, Esq.-p. 4

SAILORS, Jesse & Jane Pearin-Mar. 4, 1847, by Rev. John B. Poniter-p. 25

SANDERS, Clark & Elizabeth Holland-Jan. 2, 1840, by Rev. Arnold Moss-p. 7

SANDERS, John & Desa McGowan-Dec. 4, 1841, by Thos. Jones, Esq.-p. 12

SAPP, Benjamin & Sarah Frazier-June 11, 1840, by Rev. John Green-p. 8

SAPP, Benjamin & Fanny Holderfield-Dec. 28, 1846, by Rev. C. McGuire-p. 24

SAPP, John & Emaline Driver-Oct. 13, 1853, by Rev. W. Martin-p. 46

SAYLORS, John & Lucinda Able [Abbe]-Nov. 5, 1828-(L.P.-B.V.)

SAYLORS, John C. & Demercius Noland-Sept. 14, 1851, by Robt. Hitchcock, Esq.-p.38

SAYLORS, Leonard & Sarah Cardwell-May 29, 1847-p. 26

SCARBOROUGH, James & Phebe Sparks-Oct. 14, 1839-p. 6

SCARBROUGH, Lewis & Nancy Sapp-Mar. 19, 1839-p. 4

SCARBROUGH, Wm. & Susanna Griffin-Feb. 18, 1816, by Thos. Horne, J.P.-(L.P.-B.V.)

SCARLETT, Moses A. & Sarah Emeline Wilson-Jan. 27, 1853, by Rev. Irvin Jones-p.43

SCOGGEN, James & Sarah Londey [Lundy]-July 1, 1847-p. 26

SCOGGIN, James Walker & Miss Sarah Griggs Green-Jan. 12, 1826-Bible Record. [He was son of Rev. John, Jr., & she was dau. of Rev. John.]

SCOGGINS, John W. & Pharda [Pheraba] Malinda C. Wheeler-Aug. 20, 1851-p. 38

SCOGGIN, Woodson Phillips & Miss Mary Green-Sept. 24, 1828-Bible Record. [He was son of Rev. John, Jr., & she was dau. of Rev. John.]

SCOGGINS, Wm. & Sookey Mason-Apr. 3, 1840-p. 8

SCOTT, Henry (Colored) & Nancy Priscilla Scott (Colored)-May 18, 1853-p. 44

SCOTT, James F. & Margaret Gracey-Mar. 25, 1852, by Rev. M. Y. Brockett-p. 41

SCOTT, James M. & Elizabeth Glenn-Jan. 19, 1849-p. 31

SCOTT, Jonathan & Christiana Lundy-Apr. 17, 1851, by Rev. Wm. Goodwin-p. 37

SCURLOCK, Thos. & Ra[c]hael Gooch-Nov. 9, 1853, by Levi Jarvis, Esq.-p. 46

SEALS, Edmond & Martha Griffith-Apr. 2, 1849-p. 31

SEALS, Martin P. & Eliza Earles-Oct. 6, 1857, by John W. Mitchell, Esq.-p. 56

SEARS, John & Lucy Ann Rowland-Sept. 2, 1841, by Rev. Peter Kuykendall-p. 12
SELBY-See: TELLEY
SETTLE, T. G. & Marian L. Young-Aug. 22, 1854, by Rev. M. Y. Brockett-p. 48

SEVERANCE, Jonathan B. & Zarilda A. Bramlet-Sept. 28, 1852, by M. Y. Brockett, M. G.-p. 42

SHACKLEFORD, D. P. & A. Leathy Young-Jan. 20, 1857, by Rev. W. C. Haislip-p. 55

SHACKLEFORD, Frank & Mary Gleeson-Nov. 28, 1855, by Rev. M. Y. Brockett-p. 52

SHARP, Isaac & Michel Perkins-Mar. 28, 1844-p. 17

SHERLEY, John & Malinda Barkley-July 13, 1851, by Andrew Graham, Esq.-p. 38

SHERRELL, Joshua & Martha P. Bray-Nov. 23, 1851, by J. B. Poniter-p. 39

SHOCKLEY, Thos. & Sarah McCormick-Oct. 25, 1838, by John Gillentine, Esq.-p. 3

SHOCKLEY, Isah & Sally Mooneyham-Sept. 10, 1838-p. 3

SHOCKLEY, Peter & Manerva Miller-Mar. 28, 1854-p. 48

SHOEMAKER, Wm. & Elizabeth Graham-Apr. 14, 1848, by Wm. C. Johnson, Esq.-p. 28

SHORT, Granville & Rebecca Huddleston-Jan. 12, 1853, by Joseph D. Hyder, Esq.-
p. 43

SHORT, Seaborn & Pressia Ann Nichols-Dec. 30, 1858, by L. H. Bennett, M.G.-p. 59

SHUGART, Wm. H. & Mary Coats-Jan. 6, 1841, by Rev. J. E. Hickman-p. 10

SHUGART, Wm. H. & Nancy Brown-Nov. 17, 1850, by Rev. Miles W. McConnell-p. 36

SHUSTER, Francis M. & Martha McDaniel-June 27, 1856, by Jas. A. Knowles, Esq.-p.53

SHUSTER, Jacob & Laniza Jane Cooke-Nov. 29, 1847, by James Knowles, Esq.-p. 27

SHUTTER, John & Nancy M. Evans-July 20, 1858-p. 58

SILVA, Ella & Unity Stamps-Dec. 20, 1840-p. 10

SIMMONS, Andrew & Feraby Mitchell-Apr. 11, 1858, by John W. Mitchell, Esq.-p. 57

SIMMONS, Benjamin L. & Nancy C. Beatty-Mar. 14, 1844, by Thos. Green, Esq.-p. 17

SIMMONS, Drury & Margaret Earles-Aug. 7, 1856, by C. A. Taylor, Esq.-p. 53

SIMMONS, Francis & Nancy C. Hodge-Oct. 15, 1857, by Wm. E. Camp, Esq.-p. 56

SIMMONS, Geo. W. & Lydia Margaret McBride-Apr. 23, 1854, by C. A. Taylor, Esq.-
p. 48

SIMMONS, Jonathan & Magdalene Clenny-Sept. 15, 1849, by C. A. Taylor-p. 32

SIMMONS, John & Rebecca McMath-May 27, 1858, by John A. Templeton, Esq.-p. 58

SIMMONS, Joseph & Matilda Quarles-May 11, 1856, by Wm. Wilson, Esq.-p. 53

SIMMONS, Wm. & Susannah Adair-Aug. 10, 1848, by Creed A. Taylor, Esq.-p. 29

SIMONS, Solomon C. & Margaret Sparkman-July 6, 1852, by Joseph Gist, Esq.-p. 41

SIMPSON, James & Sarah Robison-Nov. 14, 1839-p. 6

SIMPSON, Richard & Drusilla A. Camron-Oct. 19, 1850-p. 35

SIMPSON, Wm. & Eliza Weaver-Oct. 11, 1831, by David Snodgrass, J.P.-(L.P.-B.V.)

SIMPSON, Wm. P. & Canzada Cameron-Oct. 4, 1848, by David Snodgrass, Esq.-p. 29

SIMRELL, Francis M. & Emily O. Dinges-July 15, 1849, by Rev. Wm. Jared-p. 32

SIMRILL, Wm. M. & Rebecca Little-Oct. 4, 1857, by Alexander Oliver, Esq.-p. 56

SIMS, Drury W. & Mahala Bohannon-Mar. 2, 1848, by Shadrick Price, Esq.-p. 28

SIMS, Lafayette & Narcissa S. Templeton-Nov. 7, 1854-p. 49

SIMS, Martin & Nancy McConnell-Dec. 6, 1853, by Rev. T. W. Pendergrass-p. 46

SIMS, Oliver H. P. & Eliza Jane Glenn-June 26, 1844, by Rev. Jesse Cole-p. 18

SINGLEBERRY, David & Nancy Owens-Nov. 2, 1810-(L.P.-B.V)

SLATTEN, Berry & Nancy Ann Jones-Oct. 12, 1853, by A. J. Sims, Esq.-p. 46

SLATTEN, Hillmer & Elizabeth Williams-Apr. 7, 1840, by Mathias Hutson, Esq.-p. 8

SLATTEN, Samuel D. & Lecrease Hutchings-Mar. 25, 1844, by Jesse M. Sullivan, Esq-
p. 17

SLATTON, Richard & Elizabeth Jones-Oct. 13, 1840, by Wm. Knowles, Esq.-p. 9

SLAUDER, James A. & Elizabeth Jane Frasure-July 25, 1855, by John W. Mitchell,
Esq.-p. 51

SLIGER, Wm. C. & Esther J. McConnell-Aug. 17, 1858, by Dempsey M. Southard-p. 58

SLOAN, Anderson & Malinda Wallace-Dec. 1, 1852-p. 43

SLYGER, John, Jr. & Sufiney C. Jones-Sept. 21, 1856, by Alvey Bussell, Esq.-p.54

SMALLWOOD, John & Nancy Whiteaker-July 25, 1855, by John Crook, Esq.-p. 51

SMITH, Abner C. & Martha Ann Burden-July 23, 1849-p. 32

SMITH, Benjamin & Nancy Herd-Dec. 23, 1856, by M. C. Dibrell, Esq.-p. 55

SMITH, Benjamin F. & Emily C. Leftwich-Jan. 23, 1850, by Rev. Wm. Barr-p. 23

SMITH, Brooks & Dorcas Ann Corder-May 4, 1851, by James Jackson, Esq.-p. 38

SMITH, C. G. O. & Nancy Kirk-Aug. 22, 1842, by James Knowles, Esq.-p. 13

SMITH, Daniel D. & Elizabeth Graham-May 28, 1846, by John Crook, Esq.-p. 23

SMITH, H. P. & Cynthia Greer-Mar. 14, 1858, by Rev. James H. Morgan-p. 57

SMITH, James & Mary Patton-Sept. 13, 1848, by Rev. Thos. Stone-p. 29

SMITH, James & Sally Ann Glenn-Oct. 29, 1851, by Jno. L. Grissom-p. 39

SMITH, James & Rebecca Dillion-July 30, 1858, by John A. Templeton-p. 58

SMITH, James D. & Martha Millsaps-Apr. 2, 1849, by J. W. Glenn, Esq.-p. 31

SMITH, James H. & Harriet J. Tucker-Sept. 13, 1848, by John W. Harpending, Esq.-
p. 29

SMITH, Jesse A. & Elizabeth Saylors-Feb. 18, 1858, by Alvy Bussell, Esq.-p. 57

SMITH, Joel & Nancy Moore-Nov. 20, 1823-"I do hereby certify that I did solemnize
the rights of matrimony between the within couple-in the presence of a
sufficient number of witnesses at the house of Samuel Moore. Geo. D.
Howard, J.P."-(L.P.-B.V)

SMITH, John & Elizabeth Downing-Mar. 12, 1840, by Rev. James H. Morgan-p. 8

SMITH, John & Mary A. Baker-Aug. 26, 1855, by Hayse Arnold, Esq.-p. 51

SMITH, John, Sr. & Nancy Holmes-Sept. 16, 1852, by J. W. Glenn, Esq.-p. 42

SMITH, John C. & Catharine Bradley-Mar. 19, 1840, by Geo. Defrees, Esq.-p. 8

SMITH, Noah J. & Lucy J. Scarbrough-Mar. 29, 1849-p. 31

SMITH, Robt. W. & Margaret E. Clark-Dec. 19, 1852, by Rev. J. Eichbaum-p. 43

SMITH, Sam'l. H. & Nancy McBride-Nov. 28, 1852, by David Snodgrass, Esq.-p. 43

SMITH, Thos. H. & Maria Lamb-July 1, 1841, by Wm. R. Tucker, Esq.-p. 11

SMITH, Thomas W. & Jane Hunter-Apr. 14, 1846, by Rev. Wm. Burden-p. 22

SMITH, Wm. B. & Mary Hunter-July 28, 1855-p. 51

SMITH, Wm. G. & Amanda Templeton-May 10, 1857, by Rev. W. D. Carnes-p. 55

SMITH, Wm. O. & Lucy Hollandsworth-May 15, 1838, by Rev. Ozias Denton-p. 2

SNODGRASS, David & Linnie Bradley-Mar. 8, 1846, by Richard Bradley, Esq.-p. 22

SNODGRASS, Joseph & Miss Louisa Leftwich-May 1, 1845-p. 19

SNODGRASS, Lafayette & Elizabeth C. Anderson-Dec. 22, 1853-p. 46

SNODGRASS, Robt. J. & Amand C. Officer-Jan. 17, 1849, by Rev. J. E. Hickman-p.30

SNODGRASS, Samuel & Adaliza Graves-Sept. 28, 1853, by Rev. M. Y. Brockett-p. 46

SNODGRASS, Thos. & Eliza Jane Evans-July 8, 1847-p. 26

SNODGRASS, Walter J. & Florella Cammorn-July 12, 1845, by Jno. Crook, Esq.-p. 19

SNODGRASS, Wm. G. & Rhodey Bradley-Mar. 2, 1854, by Rev. M. Y. Brockett-p. 47

SNODGRASS, Wm. James & Winnieford Norton Bradley-Dec. 28, 1853, by Rev. M. Y. Brockett-p. 47

SOUTHARD, Aaron & Mary Ann Carmichael-No date, but between Oct. 10 & 12, 1838-p. 3. [???See: Wm. C. Johnson.]

SOUTHARD, Alfred & Mary Sparks-Oct. 2, 1838, by Elisha Cameron, Esq.-p. 3

SOUTHARD, Dempsey M. & Eliza McConnell-Feb. 23, 1843, by Rev. Jesse E. Hickman-p. 15

SPARKMAN, Bryant & Sarah Ann McCrory-Feb. 26, 1840, by Rev. John H. Mann-p. 8

SPARKMAN, Bryant & Elizabeth Copeland-Feb. 22, 1847-p. 25

SPARKMAN, James R. & Phoebe Denton-Sept. 14, 1848, by Rev. Isaac Denton-p. 29

SPARKMAN, Lewis & Nancy Anderson-Nov. 7, 1839, by John Gillentine, Esq.-p. 6

SPARKMAN, Lewis & Nancy Copeland-Feb. 17, 1843, by Rev. Geo. Stubblefield-p. 15

SPARKMAN, Meredith S. & S. Adaline Holder-Feb. 19, 1857, by Rev. Thos. E. Hutson-p. 55

SPARKMAN, Oliver & Hannah G. Witt-Feb. 8, 1853, by E. W. Denton, Esq.-p. 44

SPARKMAN, Wm. & Eliza Howard-Sept. 10, 1840, by Thos. Green, Esq.-p. 9

SPARKMAN, Wm. Read & Margaret Holder-Dec. 23, 1858, by Rev. T. E. Hutson-p. 59

SPARKS, Jacob & Minerva Jay-Dec. 29, 1841-(not returned)-p. 12

SPARKS, Levi & Mary Hennessee-Feb. 19, 1850-p. 34

SPARKS, Levi & Leah Graham-Feb. 12, 1850-p. 34

SPARKS, Wm., Jr. & Rachel Lee-Mar. 30, 1851, by James Jackson, Esq.-p. 37

SPEARS, James & Nancy Dunnagan-Apr. 16, 1840-p. 8

SPERRY, Thos. L. & Mary J. Greene-Oct. 20, 1857, by Rev. M. Y. Brockett-p. 56. [Is this a double wedding? See: James H. Bryan. She was dau. of Wm. & Mary (Fryer) Green.]

SPURR, Isaac C. & Nancy Yates-July 11, 1847-p. 26

STACEY, C. Green & Mary Austin-Dec. 24, 1857, by M. C. Dibrell, Esq.-p. 57

STACEY, Green & Malinda Davis-Nov. 15, 1853, by Rev. Wm. Burden-p. 46

STACY, Isiah & Elizabeth Franks-Sept. 17, 1840, by Wm. Little, Esq.-p. 9

STAMPS, Thomas & Mary Jane Parker-Dec. 10, 1856, by J. H. Isom, Esq.-p. 54

STANLEY, Wm. & Minerva Upchurch-Mar. 18, 1849, by J. L. Grissom, Esq.-p. 31

STEEDMAN, John & Mary McCoy-Dec. 13, 1849, by Rev. Wm. Jared-p. 33

STEEL, Tilford & Elizabeth Stacy-Mar. 31, 1855-p. 50

STEPHENS, David & Armina Oxford-Dec. 14, 1852-p. 43-"No property found. Returned and wants money back but don't get it."

STEPHENSON, Brittian E. & Sarahan Fitch-Jan. 18, 1849, by Abe Saylors, Esq.-p.30

STEWART, Erion & Symena[Samantha] Cordle-Aug. 15, 1845, by John Crook, Esq.-p.19

STEWART, James M. & Arreny McEwin-Mar. 13, 1849, by Abe Saylors, Esq.-p. 31

STEWART, Jesse & Jane Glenn-Oct. 11, 1842, by Jesse M. Sullivan, Esq.-p. 14

STEWART, Jesse & Zealy D. Howard-Feb. 9, 1848-p. 27

STEWART, John W. & Sarah Stewart-Dec. 14, 1845, by Wm. Glenn, Esq.-p. 21

STEWART, Samuel & Eliza Cooper-Sept. 11, 1856, by David Snodgrass, Esq.-p. 54

STEWART, Stephen & Mary Jarvis-May 28, 1851, by Andrew J. Sims, Esq.-p. 38

STEWART, Thos. & Mary Ann Glenn-Dec. 27, 1843, by James Knowles, Esq.-p. 17

STEWART, Wm. R. & Rebecca Cody-Sept. 30, 1855, by Rev. Francis M. Hickman-p. 51

STILES, Jacob & Elizabeth Webster-Mar. 7, 1853, by David Snodgrass, Esq.-p. 44

STILES, Latin & Sarah L. Royal-Jan. 6, 1853, by Rev. J. H. Richey-p. 43

STINETT, Geo. W. & Sarah E. M. Lowell-Feb. 9, 1858-p. 57

STIPE, Jacob, Jr. & Caroline Clenny-Aug. 2, 1849, by Joseph G. Mitchell, Esq-p.32

STOCKDON, Isaack & Amanda Randals-May 26, 1840, by John Walling, Esq.-p. 8

STONE, Hiram S. & Lean Defreese-Oct. 20, 1840, by Rev. Corder Stone-p. 9

STONE, Isaac C. & Leann Weaver-May 29, 1853, by Rev. Thos. Stone-p. 45

STONE, James C. & Elizabeth J. Carmichael-Nov. 3, 1851, by Wm. C. Johnson-p. 39

STONE, John A. & Adala Bohannon-Sept. 16, 1852, by Wm. C. Bounds-p. 42

STONE, Lewis & Mary E. H. Davis-Aug. 14, 1851, by Rev. W. Martin-p. 38

STONE, William (?)H. & Eliza Jane Henry-Aug. 30, 1849, by Rev. John Julien-p.32

STREET, John & Martha Robison-Apr. 15, 1852, by A. Graham, Esq.-p. 41

STREET, Richard & Patience Randolph-Feb. 26, 1846, by David Snodgrass-p. 22

STROUD, David & Susan Jackson-Oct. 9, 1856, by Alvey Bussell, Esq.-p. 54

STRUNK, Joel & Zilly Hunter-July 18, 1851, by John Madewell, Esq.-p. 38

STRUNK, Thos. & Catharine Jackson-May 26, 1854-p. 48

SULLIVAN, James H. & Mary Kerby-Sept. 29, 1858, by Wm. I. Russell, Esq.-p. 58

SULLIVAN, Jesse M. & Elizabeth G. Watson-Oct. 9, 1839, by Richard Crowder, Esq.-
p. 6

SULLIVAN, Jesse M. & Caroline Taylor-Apr. 26, 1848, by A. L. Shaw, Esq.-p. 28

SULLIVAN, John H. & Cansada C. Cameron-Sept. 18, 1851, by R. R. Ritchey-p. 39

SULLIVAN, Michael & Nancy Clark-Jan. 24, 1859-p. 59

SULLIVAN, Pleasant L. & Charlotte Cope-Oct. 25, 1854, by Pev. L.H. Bennett-p.49

SUTTLE, Jesse & Alcy Henessee-Feb. 14, 1849-p. 31

SUTTON, James & Eliza E. Wilson-Sept. 17, 1848, by Hugh Gracy, Esq.-p. 29

SWACK, Andrew Jackson & Sarah Angeline Weaver-June 11, 1858, by David Snodgrass,
Esq.-p. 58

SWACK, Wm. A. & Margret Clark-Nov. 14, 1848, by James Jackson, Esq.-p. 30

SWAFFORD, James & Martha Wallace-Nov. 4, 1858, by Rev. James Herd-p. 59

SWIFT, Thomas J. & Louisa Pollard-Jan. 8, 1853-p. 43

SWINDELL, Christopher & Louvinia Hutson-Dec. 28, 1850-p. 36

SWINDLE, Cason & Rutha Roberts-July 9, 1843, by John Swindle, Esq.-p. 15

SWINDLE, Geo. C. & Manerva Clark-Jan. 12, 1854, by Rev. Thos. Hutson-p. 47

SWINDLE, George W. & Jane Knowles-Aug. 19, 1848, by Rev. Thos. E. Hutson-p. 29

SWINDLE, Reuben L. & Mary Jane Keathly-Nov. 4, 1852, by Rev. T. E. Hutson-p. 42

SWINDLE, Samuel C. & Tabitha Moore-Aug. 22, 1844-p. 18

SWINDLE, Washington & Eliza Ann Keathley-Dec. 12, 1855, by Rev. Thos. E. Hutson-p. 52

SWINT, Henry & Nancy Mitchell-Jan. 3, 1837-(L.P.-B.V.)

TABER, Wm. & Mary Taber-Apr. 21, 1844, by John Crook, Esq.-p. 17

TALLENT, Thos. & Letitia Menis-Feb. 21, 1854, by Rev. Wm. Jared-p. 47

TANNER, James M. & Sarah E. Beam-Jan. 18, 1853, by Rev. John Whaley-p. 43

TAYLOR, Abner & Maria A. Watson-Feb. 15, 1847-p. 25

TAYLOR, Alexander & Matilda Patton-Feb. 29, 1852, by John Crook, Esq.-p. 40

TAYLOR, Hiram W. & Martha L. Griffith-Jan. 5, 1841, by Thos. Green, Esq.-p. 10

TAYLOR, John & Susan Waters-Apr. 26, 1853-p. 44

TAYLOR, Mackin & Julia Wesson-July 17, 1849, by Wm. Clayton, Esq.-p. 32

TAYLOR, Obadiah & Mary T. Doyle-Oct. 24, 1850, by Rev. James Herd-p. 35

TEETERS, Jacob A. & Sarah Holder-NO DATE, but bet. Nov. 15 & 28, 1849-p. 33

TELLEY[SELBY], Henderson & Mary Cardwell-July 3, 1845, by Rev. B.F. Farell-p. 19

TEMPLETON, Geo. W. & Mary J. Farris-Dec. 24, 1850, by J. L. Grissom-p. 36

TEMPLETON, Greenville H. & Amaranda S. Farris-June 16, 1850, by Elijah Denton-p. 34

TEMPLETON, John A. & Helen L. Sims-Mar. 27, 1851, by Rev. R. R. Richey-p. 37

TEMPLETON, Wm. & Ann E. Chisom-Dec. 22, 1857, by E. W. Denton, Esq.-p. 57

THOMAS, John & Mary Elroad-July 18, 1847, by Rev. Levi Perkins-p. 26

THOMAS, Joshua & Elizabeth Massa-Dec. 30, 1845, by Alva Bussell, Esq.-p. 21

THOMAS, Wm. & Letha Jacobs-Feb. 24, 1840, by Rev. Arnold Moss-p. 7

THURMAN, Axley & Catharine Fite-Dec. 7, 1839, by David Snodgrass-p. 7

TIDWELL, Francis M. & Elizabeth Earles-June 28, 1855, by Wm. E. Camp, Esq.-p. 50

TITTLE, Samuel C. & Lydia Denton-Sept. 7, 1843, by Elijah W. Denton, Esq.-p. 16

TOLISON, Matison & Mary Glenn-Feb. 18, 1852, by Joseph W. Glenn, Esq.-p. 40

TOLLISON, Solomon & Malinda Martin-Sept. 8, 1853, by Rev. Wm. Goodwin-p. 45

TOMBOLIN, Isaac & Barthena Wilson-Nov. 23, 1857-p. 56

TOMBOLIN, Jeremiah & Sarah Keathly-Aug. 30, 1858-p. 58

TOMLIN, George & Rhoda Clark-Mar. 10, 1842, by Rev. Abel Hutson-p. 13

TOWNSEND, Albert & Elizabeth Hill-Jan. 31, 1839, by Isaac Buck, Esq.-p. 5

TREWITT, John A. & Jane Crook-Apr. 10, 1851, by J. B. Wynns-p. 37

TROBAUGH, Barnard & Sarah E. Charles-June 8, 1858, by Rev. M. Y. Brockett-p. 58

TROBAUGH, James & Nancy Jackson-Jan. 26, 1857-p. 55

TROGDEN, Albert Lee & Phebe Blankenship-July 12, 1853, by Wm. Woods-p. 45

TROUGHBOCK, James & Josephine Southard-Mar. 21, 1856-p. 53

TUCKER, Carrol & Jane Frasier-Aug. 26, 1846, by M. C. Dibrell-p. 23

TUCKER, Henry L. & Elizabeth Beasley-Mar. 23, 1839-p. 4

TUCKER, John R. & Malinda Hitchcock-Jan. 18, 1840, by Rev. Levi Perkins-p. 7

TURNER, Hadley & Elizabeth Turner-Mar. 21, 1839, by Elijah Frost, Esq.-p. 5

TURNER [TURNEY?], Howard & Sarah E. Roberts-Aug. 15, 1843, by John Swindle, Esq.-
p. 16

TURNER, Mark & Elizabeth Earles-July 6, 1858, by E. W. Denton, Esq.-p. 58

TURNEY, Haywood & Margarett Davis-Dec. 18, 1851-p. 39

(?)TURNEY, Peter & Elizabeth Cummings-Feb. 1, 1859-p. 59

UNDERWOOD, Elijah C. & Rebecca Clenny-Dec. 25, 1842, by Thos. Green, Esq.-p. 14

UPCHURCH, Enoch S. & Louisa A. Shuster-July 30, 1846, by Rev. Arnold Moss-p. 23

USREY, John M. & Nancy Deweese-June 8, 1848-p. 29

USREY, Thos. C. & Leitha Jane Moore-Aug. 3, 1851, by J. W. Glenn, Esq.-p. 38

USREY, Wm. & Eliza Jane Bynum-Sept. 26, 1843, by Robt. H. McManus, Esq.-p. 16

VADEN, Smith & Elinder Jones-Nov. 27, 1840, by Wm. Knowles, Esq.-p. 9

VANDEVER, Charles & Lucinda Randalls-Aug. 5, 1847, by Thos. Cooper, Esq.-p. 26

VANDEVER, Elihu & Mary Hunter-June 8, 1841-(not returned)-p. 11

VANDEVER, Eli N. & Elcy England-Oct. 26, 1850, by W. R. Tucker, Esq.-p. 36

VANDEVER, Thomas & Sarah Tallent-Feb. 8, 1846, by Alvey Bussell, Esq.-p. 22

VANDIVER, Elihew & Theresa Conley-Mar. 22, 1854, by Rich. Bradley, Esq.-p. 47

VANDIVER, Thomas & Mary Hunter-June 14, 1841-(not returned)-p. 11

VANDIVER, Wm. & Edith Mitchell-June 10, 1841, by David Snodgrass, Esq.-p. 11

VANTREESE, Levi D. & Sarah Haynes-Jan. 31, 1850-p. 34

VAN WINKLE, James P. & Sarah Ann Thomas-Apr. 13, 1853, by Rev. W. Martin-p. 44

VAN WINKLE, Thos. & Caroline Dyer-Jan. 23, 1851, by Rev. R. A. Forest-p. 36

VAN WINKLE, Wiley R. & Matilda Howard-Mar. 3, 1851-p. 37

VASS, Alexander & Mary Gracey-Mar. 30, 1854, by Rev. M. Y. Brockett-p. 47

VATCH, Phillip & Susanah Duke-Apr. 6, 1841, by Rev. J. H. Morgan-p. 11

VAUGHN, John & Martha Young-May 11, 1839-p. 5

VAUGHN, John & Nancy Adcock-Jan. 17, 1846, by Thos. Jones, Esq.-p. 22

VICKERY, Hiram & Polly Harmon-Nov. 3, 1849-p. 32

VINCENT, Isaac M. & Louisa Maulden-Oct. 26, 1853, by Rev. Wm. Jared-p. 46

VOLEVRY, Charles & Margaret Horsly-Nov. 23, 1848, by James Webb, Esq.-p. 30

VOLIVA, James & Elizabeth M. Rodgers-Nov. 30, 1843, by Rev. Isaac C. Woodward-p. 16

WADDLE, Henry & Martha Worley-Nov. 11, 1857, by Wm. I. Russell, Esq.-p. 56

WADE, Wm. S. & Somancey Evans-Dec. 31, 1851, by Wm. Clayton, Esq.-p. 40

WALDEN, Terry, Jr. & Louisa Doyle-Feb. 15, 1844, by Wm. Austin, Esq.-p. 17

WALKER, Absolom & Jane Baldwin-July 9, 1855, by Richard Simpson, Esq.-p. 50

WALKER, Bennet & Elizabeth A. Ussery-Dec. 4, 1845, by John Wilhite, Esq.-p. 21

WALKER, John D. & Eliza Turner-Jan. 10, 1839, by Asa Certain-p. 4

WALKER, John M. B. & Mary A. Frost-Jan. 26, 1854, by John Crook, Esq.-p. 47

WALKER, Rezia & Pherebe England-Jan. 15, 1852, by Samuel Usrey, Esq.-p. 40

WALKER, Stephen F. & Mary Ann Braddock-Nov. 9, 1854, by John Crook, Esq.-p. 49

WALKER, Wm. & Polly McClain-Aug. 29, 1847, by M. C. Dibrell, Esq.-p. 26

WALKER, Wm. & Ruth Elizabeth Morrow-Oct. 12, 1854, by John Crook, Esq.-p. 49

WALKER, Wm. G. & Martha Tanner-Mar. 30, 1854, by John Crook, Esq.-p. 47

WALKER, Wm. H. & Ann Graham-Oct. 2, 1851, by Andrew Graham-p. 39

WALLACE, Laban, Jr. & Rachael Mitchell-Nov. 30, 1852, by Rev. Wm. _____-p. 43

WALLACE, Mathew H. & Emeline Hampton-Aug. 11, 1845, by Thos. Green, Esq.-p. 19

WALLER, John & Mary Womack-Oct. 6, 1852, by Wm. R. Tucker, Esq.-p. 42

WALLING, Daniel, Jr. & Rebecca Gist-Aug. 25, 1842, by Wm. Austin, Esq.-p. 13

WALLING, James & Altemira Pennington-Jan. 3, 1839, by Rev. Ozias Denton-p. 4

WALLING, James & Martha Howard-Nov. 14, 1843, by Wm. Austin, Esq.-p. 16 .

WALLING, James, Senr. & Miss Mary Defreese-Dec. 30, 1845, by Wm. Glenn, Esq.-p.21

WALLING, Jesse & Susan Roberts-Feb. 19, 1843, by John Swindle, Esq.-p. 15

WALLING, Joseph H. & Nancy M. Cope-Nov. 28, 1849, by Rev. Isaac Denton-p. 33

WALLING, Ozias & Roda Ann Pennington-Feb. 16, 1841, by Jesse Walling, Esq.-p. 10

WALLING, Ozias D. & Susannah Herd-July 21, 1839, by Anderson Rogers, Esq.-p. 5

WALLING, Thomas & Martha Gist-Mar. 16, 1841, by Jesse Walling, Esq.-p. 11

WALLING, Thomas R. & Martha Denton-May 19, 1840, by Rev. Arnold Moss-p. 8

WALLING, William & Caroline Russell-July 16, 1840, by Jesse Walling, Esq.-p. 9

WALLIS [WALLACE], John & Dicy P. White-Feb. 24, 1847-p. 25. [She was dau. of
        John & Adelphia (Doyle) White, Jr.]

WALLIS [WALLACE], John & Jane Ramsey-Nov. 16, 1853-p. 46. [In 1850 census, she
        was living with John & Elizabeth (White) Scoggin.]

WARD, M. A. & Mary Elizabeth Elms-Apr. 13, 1854, by Richard Bradley, Esq.-p. 48

WARREN, Bluford & Sarah Gracy-Dec. 8, 1849-p. 33

WATSON, Arthur & Manerva Prince-Sept. 19, 1851, by Creed A. Taylor-p. 39

WATSON, David & Susan Walling-Aug. 8, 1840, by John Jett, Esq.-p. 7

WATSON, David & Matilda Rogers-Nov. 29, 1849, by C. A. Taylor, Esq.-p. 33

WATSON, John & Sarah Jane Taylor-Nov. 5, 1843-p. 16

WATSON, John & Mary Baker-Aug. 21, 1850-p. 35

WEATHERFORD, Bloomfield & Sarah Scott-Mar. 17, 1850-p. 34

WEATHERFORD, James & Catherine Bowman-Dec. 23, 1840-p. 10

WEAVER, Benjamin, Jr. & Rhoda Ann Brumbalow-Sept. 14, 1851, by Andrew Graham-p.38

WEAVER, Joel & Salina Dearing-Aug. 5, 1851, by Andrew Graham, Esq.-p. 38

WEAVER, John J. & Leann McBride-Dec. 25, 1845, by Solomon Yeager, Esq.-p. 21

WEAVER, John P. D. & Oma McCully-Sept. 17, 1848, by Wm. C. Johnson, Esq.-p. 29

WEAVER, Thos. J. & Louisa Marrs-Nov. 22, 1847-p. 27

WEBB, Alfred & Mary Gist-Mar. 24, 1851-p. 37

WEBB, Alfred S. & Altazarle W. Officer-Oct. 5, 1848, by Rev. S. B. Lyles-p. 29

WEBB, Austin & M. J. Berch-Jan. 9, 1851, by J. B. Lyles-p. 36

WEBB, Crockett D. & Nancy Jane Webb-Apr. 2, 1857, by Rev. T. E. Hutson-p. 55

WEBB, Edward & Elizabeth Burden [Burton]-Oct. 16, 1813, by Joseph Cummings, J.P.-
        (L.P.-B.V.)

WEBB, Elisha & Harriet Jane Little-Dec. 15, 1840-p. 10

WEBB, Elisha & Emily Lewis-Oct. 9, 1850-p. 35

WEBB, Finley D. & Catherine P. Officer-Aug. 28, 1847-p. 26

WEBB, James & Nancy Holland-Jan. 23, 1840, by Wm. Knowles, Esq.-p. 7

WEBB, Jeremiah & Edith Denton-Mar. 30, 1858, by Elijah W. Denton-p. 57

WEBB, Jeremiah, Jr. & Amanda Sparkman-Dec. 26, 1855, by Rev. Thos. E. Hutson-p.52

WEBB, Westley & Manerva Moore-Feb. 15, 1847-p. 25

WEBSTER, Joshua & Nancy King-Dec. 19, 1847, by Joseph Gist, Esq.-p. 27

WEBSTER, Joshua & Amanda Passons-Sept. 22, 1852, by Rev. Jas. H. Morgan-p. 42

WELCH, Archibald & Rebecca Sluder-Jan. 4, 1855, by John W. Mitchell, Esq.-p. 49

WELCH, James & Mary T. Fox-Jan. 17, 1859, by Richard Simpson, Esq.-p. 59

WEST, Andrew J. & Mary Ann Dearing -Jan. 26, 1854, by Rev. Elijah Hale-p. 47

WEST, Paris & Alice Bohannon-Dec. 29, 1849-p. 33

WESTON, David & Ann Jones-June 19, 1850-p. 34

WETHERFORD, Memory & Ester Bennett-Mar. 20, 1844, by Wm. Glenn, Esq.-p. 17

WHEELER, Thomas L. & Martha A. Slyger-Oct. 28, 1852-p. 42

WHITAKER, James & Nancy Henry-June 13, 1839, by Jas. Bartlett, Esq.-p. 6

WHITAKER, Leroy & Sarah Whitaker-June 1, 1848, by John Madewell, Esq.-p. 28

WHITAKER, Pleasant & Margaret Whitaker-Mar. 1, 1849, by J. D. Hyder, Esq.-p. 31

WHITE, Benjamin & Hetty Whitley-Aug. 2, 1852, by Rev. J. H. Morgan-p. 42

WHITE, Benjamin & Jane Smith-Aug. 21, 1856, by Hayes Arnold, Esq.-p. 53

WHITE, Edmund Russell & Sarah Rogers-July 1, 1854-p. 48

WHITE, James & Elizabeth Martin-Mar. 14, 1853, by Isaac Lollar, Esq.-p. 44

WHITE, John C. M. & Maria Lucy Thomas-Sept. 15, 1853, by Rev. Wm. Martin-p. 45

WHITE, John D. & Margaret Taylor-Oct. 12, 1846-p. 24

WHITE, Martin & Mary White-Aug. 16, 1857, by Rev. Wm. D. Carnes-p. 56. [She was dau. of John, Jr., & unrelated to her husband.]

WHITE, Milton R. & Susan Herd-Feb. 18, 1846, by Rev. Isaac Denton-p. 22. [He was son of John, Jr.]

WHITE, Robert & Betsy German-July 30, 1825-(L.P.-B.V.)

WHITE, Simon [Doyle] & Delilea Wallace-Dec. 18, 1845, by Rev. David Coulson-p.21. [He was son of John, Jr.]

WHITE, Simon D. & Martha E[veline] May-Sept. 26, 1853-p. 46.

WHITE, Wm. L[ove] & Lucinda F. Turney-Jan. 9, 1849, by Rev. S. L. Summar-p. 30. [He was son of Woodson Phillips & Nancy (Mitchell) White.]

WHITE, Woodson P[hillips] & Nancy Mitchell-Sept. 11, 1810-Bible Record. [He was son of John White, Sr., Revol. soldier, & his wife, Martha Phillips. This marriage may have taken place in N. C., as census records show that their first child, Dyer P., was b. 1811, in N. C.]

WHITEACRE, David & Miss Mary Henderson-Sept. 24, 1845, by Rev. Thos. Stone-p. 19

WHITEAKER, Henry & Edith Cash-Dec. 22, 1846-p. 24

WHITEFIELD, Josiah & Dicy R. Perkins-Dec. 15, 1839, by Geo. Defrees, Esq.-p. 7

WHITEFIELD, Thos. & Mary Conoy-Aug. 24, 1848-p. 29

WHITLEY, John M. & Margaret Downey-Jan. 23, 1853, by Sam'l. Usrey, Esq.-p. 43

WHITLY, Wm. H. & Martha Lewis-June 3, 1858, by M. C. Dibrell, Esq.-p. 58

WHITSON, James & Elizabeth Cook-Oct. 4, 1838, by Elisha Cameron, Esq.-p. 3

WHITSON, James & Matilda Broyles-June 14, 1847-p. 26

WHITSON, Ruben & Margrett Dyer-Aug. 17, 1847-p. 26

WIGGINS, Aaron & Hellen Swift-Oct. 20, 1840, by James Knowles, Esq.-p. 9

WIGGINS, Adolphus & Clarinda McPhearson-Nov. 23, 1853, by Abram Saylors-p. 46

WIGGINS, Joseph & Malinda Marlow-Oct. 20, 1858, by Jno. A. Templeton-p. 58

WIGINGTON, William & Elizabeth Hensley-Dec. 3, 1858, by David Snodgrass, Esq.-p.59

WILHITE, Christopher & Jane Farley-Mar. 9, 1840-p. 8

WILHITE, Christopher & Elizabeth Farley-Jan. 31, 1841, by John Pennington-p. 10

WILHITE, Elias & Catherine Pass-Dec. 19, 1838, by Rev. J. E. Hickman-p. 4

WILHITE, Elias & Martha J. Whitson-June 2, 1853, by David Snodgrass-p. 44

WILHITE, John & Susannah Deweese-Sept. 19, 1847, by John Wilhite, Esq.-p. 26

WILHITE, Reuben & Julian Wisdom-May 9, 1839, by Rev. J. E. Hickman-p. 5

WILHITE, Reuben & Pollyan Barrans-Mar. 19, 1849-p. 31

WILHITE, Wm. & Jane Bennett-July 31, 1844, by Wm. Glenn, Esq.-p. 18

WILHITE, Wm. & Anney Henrey-June 27, 1845, by Rev. Thos. Stone-p. 22

WILHITE, Wm. & Mary Mayberry-Sept. 11, 1849, by J. W. Glenn, Esq.-p. 32

WILKER, Willie W. & Mary M. Farmington-June 13, 1835-(L.P.-B.V.)

WILLHITE, Isaac A. & Aralissa Howard-Aug. 2, 1855, by Rev. Thos. Stone-p. 51

WILLHITE, Leonard & America Julien-Aug. 16, 1851, by Wm. C. Johnson-p. 38

WILLIAMS, Andrew J. & Mary Louisa Butram-Oct. 31, 1858, by Rich. Bradley, Esq.-
p. 59

WILLIAMS, Chaucer & Sarah Jane Buttram-Mar. 12, 1845-p. 19

WILLIAMS, Chaucey N. & Nelley Miller-July 3, 1852, by Wm. C. Johnson, Esq.-p. 41

WILLIAMS, Dennis C. & Lucinda Medcalf-Sept. 18, 1839-p. 6

WILLIAMS, Jackson & Mary Jane Collins-Dec. 2, 1852, by David Snodgrass, Esq.-p.43

WILLIAMS, Jerimiah & Frances Holman-Mar. 2, 1843, by Richd. Bradley, Esq.-p. 15

WILLIAMS, Jesse S[coggin] & Elizabeth Tate-May 15, 1844, by Wm. Austin, Esq.-p.
18. [He was son of James & Hannah (Scoggin) & she was dau. of Vincent
B. & Sallie (Whiteside).]

WILLIAMS, John & Mary L. Geer-Dec. 25, 1845, by Rev. Levi Perkins-p. 21

WILLIAMS, Madison & Sarah Young-June 8, 1848, by Rev. Wm. Burden-p. 29

WILLIAMS, Marion & Louisa Ann Goodwin-July 1, 1854-p. 48

WILLIAMSON, Elisha C. & Nancy Templeton-Aug. 24, 1852, by Waman L. Woods, Esq.-
p. 42

WILLIAMSON, W. G. & Nancy Sewell-Oct. 24, 1852, by Rev. T. E. Hutson-p. 42

WILLIS, James & Elizabeth Certain-Sept. 25, 1839-p. 6

WILLIS, John & Eliza Feltz-June 26, 1856, by John L. Grissom, Esq.-p. 53

WILLMETH, James & Martha Clouse-Sept. 13, 1847-p. 26

WILMOUTH, John & Shelin Blackburn-Jan. 4, 1840-p. 7

WILSON, Alfred & Mary Dodson-Dec. 23, 1838, by John Gillentine, Esq.-p. 4

WILSON, Gilmore & Margarett Mason-Sept. 11, 1839, by James Knowles-p. 5

WILSON, Green & Susan Swindle-Jan. 30, 1859, by John A. Templeton, Esq.-p. 59

WILSON, Green & Lucinda Howard-Oct. 28, 1858, by Rev. Thos. Stone-p. 59

WILSON, Greenville & Elizabeth Greenfield-Aug. 18, 1842, by James Knowles, Esq.-
p. 13

WILSON, Hartwell G. & Mary M. Dale-Apr. 26, 1841-(not returned)-p. 11

WILSON, James C. & Margarett M. Grasty-Mar. 16, 1848-p. 28

WILSON, James H. & Amy Scoggins-June 3, 1841-(not returned)-p. 11

WILSON, James R. & Ruth Shockley-May 20, 1855, by John W. Mitchell, Esq.-p. 50

WILSON, Mumford & Elizabeth M. Dodson-Jan. 12, 1852-p. 40

WILSON, Nathaniel & Nancy Parker Davis-May 31, 1853, by Rev. Wm. Goodwin-p. 44

WILSON, Phillip B. & Emaline Lowery-Jan. 29, 1850-p. 34

WILSON, Ruben & Nancy Glenn-Sept. 4, 1845, by David Snodgrass, Esq.-p. 19

WILSON, Samuel & Polly Ann Manes-Oct. 19, 1854, by Abram Saylors, Esq.-p. 49

WILSON, Spencer & Emaline Felton-Mar. 19, 1853, by Rev. Wm. Burden-p. 44

WILSON, Spencer & Martha Boyd-Dec. 27, 1855, by Rev. Wm. Boyd-p. 52

WILSON, Wm. & Miss Sarah Green-Dec. 2, 1845, by Rev. Ozias Denton-p. 21

WILSON, Wm. & Margaret Foster-Feb. 22, 1854, by Richmond Frasure-p. 47

WILSON, Young & Absley Jacobs-Jan. 10, 1840, by Rev. Arnold Moss-p. 7

WINDERS, James & Paulina Lowrey-Aug. 21, 1857, by Wm. R. Tucker, Esq.-p. 56

WINDERS, John & Susan Kerby-Aug. 17, 1857, by John J. Duncan, Esq.-p. 56

WINSTEAD, Ephraim & Mary Ann Pirtle-July 24, 1856, by John L. Grissom, Esq.-p.53

WISEINER, Alexander & Polly Dukes-Oct. 20, 1847, by James Herd, Sr., M.G.-p. 27

WITT, Allison & Eliza M. Yeager-Oct. 10, 1847, by Solomon Yeager, Esq.-p. 27

WITT, Charles W. & Phebe Emaline Yeager-Nov. 10, 1842, by Rev. Jesse E. Hickman-p. 14

WITT, Thomas H. & Martha McElroy-Mar. 2, 1848, by E. W. Denton, Esq.-p. 28

WITTEN, Thomas & Leacy Marr-Nov. 6, 1845, by Wm. W. Rose-p. 21

WOMACK, Wm. & Celia Tombolin-Jan. 9, 1849, by J. L. Grisham, Esq.-p. 30

WOMACK, Wm. A. & Matilda Davis-Sept. 30, 1852, by T. E. Hutson-p. 42

WOOD, John J. & Elizabeth Bartlett-Apr. 15, 1849, by J. D. Hyder-p. 31

WOODS, Waman & Nancy Anderson-Sept. 20, 1848, by Rev. W. H. Hooker-p. 29

WOODS, Wm. C. & Margaretta B. Simpson-Sept. 9, 1851, by Rev. J. H. Morgan-p. 38

WOOTEN, Elijah, Jr. & Jane Vest-Feb. 27, 1850, by Wm. Clayton, Esq.-p. 34

WORLEY, Allen A. & Martha Dodson-Mar. 2, 1849-p. 31

WORLEY, Henry M. & Ann Presley-Sept. 25, 1851, by Joseph G. Mitchell, Esq.-p. 39

WORLEY, Isaac & Nancy Worley-Dec. 8, 1853, by Rev. James Herd-p. 46

WORLEY, Joshua & Eliza Underwood-Apr. 10, 1857-p. 55

WORLEY, Milton R. & Margarett Campbell-Oct. 6, 1842, by Thos. Green, Esq.-p. 14

WORLEY, Milton R. & Margaret Graham-July 15, 1853-p. 45

WORLEY, Milton R. & Sarah Brazeal-May 8, 1856, by John W. Mitchell, Esq.-p. 53

WORLEY, Milton R. & Sarah Cecil-Jan. 12, 1859, by John W. Mitchell, Esq.-p. 59

WORLEY, Moses & Creda Worley-May 28, 1853, by Rev. Jas. H. Morgan-p. 45

WORLEY, William & Sarah Worley-Nov. 13, 1839, by Anderson S. Rogers-p. 6

WORLEY, Wm. & Sarah Quarles-July 12, 1858, by Wm. Wilson, Esq.-p. 58

WORLEY, Wm. P. & Lucretia Worley-July 3, 1856, by Wm. Clayton, Esq.-p. 53

WYCOUGH, Sidney & Sarah Ann Bennett-Jan. 13, 1853, by J. B. Lowrey-p. 43

WYNN, Joseph B. & Mary N. Johnston-Oct. 31, 1843, by Rev. Amos M. Stone-p. 16

YAGER, William W. & Elizabeth Dearing-July 17, 1841, by David Snodgrass, Esq.-p.11

YARBROUGH, George & Celia Davis-Sept. 15, 1839, by Elijah Frost, Esq.-p. 6

YATES, Alfred & Sarah Ramsey-Sept. 24, 1843, by Anderson S. Rogers, Esq.-p. 16

YATES, Eli & Eliza B. Lewis-Aug. 9, 1838, by Thos. Green, Esq.-p. 2

YATES, Geo. W. & Mary Walling-Dec. 17, 1850-p. 36

YATES, Geo. W. & Elizabeth Godard-Apr. 15, 1856, by E. W. Denton, Esq.-p. 53

YATES, John, Jr. & Sarah A. Baker-Mar. 5, 1851-p. 37

YATES, Raleigh W. & Louisa Hill-Oct. 30, 1850-p. 36

YATES, Wm. & Sarah A. Warren-Sept. 10, 1847-p. 26

YEAGER, Daniel W. & Susan Hambleton-Oct. 14, 1845, by Rev. Jesse E. Hickman-p.21

YEAGER, Lemuel A. & Louisa Robinson-Nov. 29, 1846-p. 24

YEAGER, Solomon & Mira J. Mitchell-Jan. 12, 1849, by Wm. C. Johnson, Esq.-p. 30

YEAGER, Solomon, Sr. & Rheby Hamblin-Dec. 14, 1848, by David Snodgrass, Esq.-p.30

YEATS, Alexander & Samira Jones-Jan. 27, 1858, by John W. Mitchell-p. 57

YEATS, Alfred & Elizabeth Jones-Feb. 8, 1857, by John W. Mitchell, Esq.-p. 55

YOUNG, Austin C. & Lucetty Clark-Nov. 5, 1840, by Rev. J. E. Hickman-p. 9

YOUNG, James & Patsey Young-June 7, 1840, by Thos. Jones, Esq.-p. 9

YOUNG, Pleasant & Polly Adcock-Mar. 10, 1846, by Thos. Jones, Esq.-p. 22

YOUNG, Robert S. & Rachel Brown-May 5, 1840, by Rev. Jesse E. Hickman-p. 8

YOUNG, Wm. & Eliza Walling-July 4, 1855-p. 50

YOUNG, Wm. M. & Matilda Wallis [Wallace]-Dec. 1, 1842, by Rev. Jesse E. Hickman-
p. 14

# BRIDES INDEX

_____, Nancy: 29
_____, Nancy T.: 51
ABLE [ABBE], Lucinda: 58
ADAIR, Margarett: 1
, Minney: 2
, Susannah: 59
ADAMS, Linda: 7
, Margrett: 55
, Sarah: 7
ADCOCK, Alcy: 39
, ELINDA: 13
, Nancy: 67
, Polly: 75
ADKINS, Malinda: 18
ALBERT, Martha C.: 19
ALBRIGHT, Izabella A.: 21
ALEXANDER, Ruth: 35
ALLEN, Mary Ann: 15
, Mary C.: 38
ALLISON, Elizabeth: 7
ANDERSON, Eliza J.: 24
, Elizabeth: 1
, Elizabeth C.: 62
, Emily: 41
, Evaline: 54
, Mahala: 20
, Margaret: 18, 21, 25
, Marteela: 55
, Martha: 40
, Mary: 3
, Nancy: 62, 73
, Peggy: 40
, Rachel: 5
, Rebecca: 36, 47
, Sarah S.: 49
ANDREWS, Nancy D.: 7
ARMSTRONG, Mrs. Mary: 14
ARNOLD, Amanda M.: 52
, Lucinda: 15
ATKINSON, Susannah: 13
AURS, Rosery: 33
AUSTIN, Emaline: 18
, Mary: 33, 63
, Susan: 19
BADGER, Mary: 14
BAILEY, Julia Ann B.: 31
BAKER, Mrs. Caroline: 2
, Elizabeth W.: 20
, Evaline: 20

BAKER, Hila: 51
, Jane: 18
, Jistin: 49
, Mary: 69
, Mary A.: 61
, Nancy: 13, 25
, Nancy Ann: 10
, Sarah A.: 74
BALDWIN, Jane: 67
BARKLEY: BARCLAY
, Malinda: 59
, Mary: 38
BARNES, Amanda: 52
, Dorcas: 23
, Elleanor: 8
, Lydia: 52
, Nancy Caroline: 15
BARR, Sally: 26
BARRANS, Pollyan: 71
BARTLETT, Elizabeth: 73
, Hester: 8
BEAM, Sarah E.: 65
BEAN, Catharine Malinda: 19
, Jude: 55
BEAR, Lucinda: 9
BEASLEY, Elizabeth: 66
BEAT(T)Y, Margaret: 14
, Nancy C.: 59
BELCHER, Lucretia: 9
BENNETT, Ester: 70
, Jane: 71
, Martha F.: 38
, Mary: 37
, Sarah Ann: 74
BENTON, Celia: 5
, Martha: 17
BERCH, M. J.: 69
BERRY, Nancy: 57
, Phila Ann: 44
, Ruth: 14
BESHEARS, Bethiah: 52
, Mary Ann: 10
, Melinda: 54
BIDWELL, Charlotte: 43
, Eliza: 43
BILLINGS, Nancy: 9
BILLINGSLY, Camelia: 48
, Permelia: 48
BLACKBURN, Elizabeth: 27

-77-

BLACKBURN: Shelin: 72
BLALOCK, Faney Jane: 5
, Rachel: 2
BLANKENSHIP, Elizabeth: 3
, Elizabeth Ann: 46
, Frances Maria: 19
, Manerva: 55
, Phebe: 66
BOGARTH, Sarah: 56
BOHAN(N)ON, Adala: 64
, Alice: 70
, Arazilla: 8
, Becah: 43
, Brunetta: 15
, Elizabeth: 23, 50
, Jane: 56
, Lucinda: 50
, Mahala: 49, 60
, (Miss) Martha: 34
, Mary: 50
, Nancy: 50
BOULDEN, Tlithea: 7
BOUNDS, Louisa: 36
, Luraney: 51
, Ruth A.: 8
BOWMAN, Catherine: 69
, Mary Ann: 7
, Milda J.: 21
, Nancy: 32
, Sarah M.: 47
BOYD, Martha: 73
, Mary Jane: 51
, Paulina: 39
BOZEARTH, Mary Ann: 36
BRADDOCK, Mary Ann: 68
BRADFORD, Elizabeth: 52 (2)
, Lincinda: 32
, Margaret: 51
, Nancy J.: 48
BRADLEY, Catharine: 61
, Elizabeth: 38
, Linnie: 61
, Rhodey: 62
, Sarah C.: 7
, Winnieford Norton: 62
BRADSHAW, Helen M.: 2
BRAMLETT, Jane A.: 3
, Zarilda A.: 58
BRAY, Eliza Ann: 3
, Martha P.: 59
, Mary Ann: 27
BRAZEALE, Eliza: 20

BREAZEAL, Sarah: 74
BREWSTER, Mary L.: 40
BRIGHT, Frances: 14
BRITTAIN, Mary: 41
BROCK, Nancy: 23
BRONSON, Hester C.: 19
BROOKS, Elizabeth: 25
, Nancy E.: 18
BROWN, Amy: 10
, Caroline: 22
, Eliza J.: 30
, Jane: 38
, Louisa: 16
, Martha: 1
, Mary: 43
, Mary C.: 20
, Mary Jane: 44
, Nancy: 43, 59
, Naoma: 9
, Rachel: 75
, Sarah Jane: 20
, Winney: 56
BROYLES, Caroline: 21
, Elizabeth: 29
, Jane: 22, 27
, Julia A.: 32
, Louisa: 49
, Lucinda: 9
, Matilda: 71
, Nancy: 16
, Olley: 36
, Sarah E.: 20
, Wincy: 57
BRUMBALOW, Rhoda Ann: 69
BRUSTER, Kitty: 27
BRYAN, Eliza: 21
, Elizabeth J.: 49
, Mahala: 46
, Martha: 41
, Martha Jane: 3
, Mary: 7
, Minerva: 24
, Sarah: 44
, Susan: 57
BRYANT, Margaret: 30
, Rebecca: 46
BUCK, Margaret: 45
BUCKNER, Mary Ann: 39
BUNCH, Amanda M.: 42
BURDEN: BURTON, Charlotte: 6
, Elizabeth: 69
, Martha Ann: 60

CONLEY, Theresa: 67
CONOY, Mary: 71
COOK, (Miss) Adaline: 22
, Elizabeth: 71
COOKE, Laniza Jane: 59
COOPER, Eliza: 63
, Judde: 54
, Lucy Ann: 54
, Mary: 21, 54
, Sarah: 34
COPE, Catharine: 41
, Charlotte: 31, 64
, Mary E.: 5
, Matilda: 36
, Nancy: 14
, Nancy M.: 68
, Sarah: 42
, Susan: 55
COPELAND, Cynthia C.: 40
, Elizabeth: 62
, Ellen: 57
, Mahala: 56
, (Miss) May: 4
, Nancy: 62
, Sarah E.: 41
CORBIT, Malviny: 21
CORDER, Dorcas Ann: 60
, Mary Jane: 5
CORDLE, Samantha: 63
, Symena: 63
COUCH, Eliza: 51
, Melonia: 12
, Susan F.: 47
COX, Mary: 1
CRAIN, Emily: 37
, Mary Ann: 5
, Salila: 45
CRAWLEY, Martha: 41
CRESON, Mary Ann: 49
CROOK, Elizabeth H.: 38
, Jane: 66
, Mary: 43
, Mary A.: 9
CROWDER, Martha: 11
, Mary: 10
CUMMINGS, Elizabeth: 66
, Jane: 6
, Sarah: 42
CUNNINGHAM, Charlotte: 1
, Eliza: 13
, Margaret: 27
DALE, Eliza: 3

DALE, Julian: 18
, Mary M.: 72
DALTON, Nancy: 27
DANIEL, Polly: 54
DAVIS, Catherine: 21
, Celia: 74
, Elizabeth: 11
, Lucinda A. C.: 34
, Malinda: 6, 24, 63
, Margarett: 66
, Martha: 1
, Mary: 3, 44, 48
, (Miss) Mary Ann: 1
, Mary E. H.: 64
, Matilda: 73
, Nancy Parker: 73
, Rebecca: 43
, Susan: 6
DAVY, Matilda: 35
DEARING, Elizabeth: 74
, Hannah: 8
, Mary Ann: 70
, Salina: 69
, Talitha A.: 13
DEFREESE, Lean: 64
, (Miss) Mary: 68
, Nancy: 2
DELAFIELD, Martha E.: 11
DENNY, Mary: 10
DENTON, Amanda: 46
, Edith: 69
, Elizabeth: 55
, Emeline: 18
, Lucinda S. F.: 22
, Lydia: 66
, Martha: 25, 68
, Martha Ann: 56
, Mary: 2
, Nancy: 25
, Pheby: 25
, Phoebe: 25
, Sara(h): 2, 25(2)
, Susan: 6
, Susan Ann: 39
DEW, Sophronia: 11
DEWEESE, Amanda: 48
, Eliza Jane: 10
, Nancy: 66
, Susannah: 71
DIBRELL, Lucinda A.: 30
DICKERSON, Louisa: 7
, Martha: 52

DICKINSON, Elizabeth: 4
DILDINE, Mary: 34
, Nancy: 44
DILLION, Olevy: 11
, Rebecca: 61
DINGES, Emily O.: 60
, Mary E.: 29
DITTY, Elizabeth: 54
, Mary: 54
, Susan: 48
DIXON, Polly: 45
, Rebecca: 35
DODSON, Eliza: 23
, Elizabeth M.: 73
, Jane A.: 53
, Malinda: 53
, Martha: 73
, Mary: 17, 72
, Susannah: 23
DOTSON, Lydia M.: 52
DOWNEY, Arabella: 36
, Margaret: 71
DOWNING, Elizabeth: 61
DOYLE, Amanda: 45
, Jane E.: 27
, Louisa: 67
, Malvina: 31
, Martha: 27
, Mary T.: 65
, Pamela: 31
, Sarah E.: 30
, Susan: 12
DRIVER, Elizabeth: 20
, Emaline: 58
, Mary Ann: 37
DUDLEY, Sarah: 42
DUKE(S), Edey: 16
, Nancy: 57
, Polly: 73
, Susanah: 67
DUNAWAY, Elizabeth: 23
DUNCAN, Hannah: 46
, Jerusha: 32
, Mary: 17
, Susannah: 37, 46
DUNN, Elizabeth: 47
, Margarett: 14
, Martha: 45
, Mary: 4
, Mary Ann: 11
, Mary Jane: 38
, Susan: 18

DUNNAGAN, Nancy: 62
DYER, Allisinia: 17
, Alvira: 26
, Caroline: 67
, Elizabeth: 33
, Louisa: 16
, Margrett: 71
EARLES, Edith: 56
, Eliza: 58
, Elizabeth: 66(2)
, Margaret: 59
, Mary Caroline: 17
, Mary R.: 1
, Nancy: 11
, Polly: 28
, Sarah: 19
, Sarah Ann: 18
EASTLAND, Martha J.: 38
, Mary Ann E.: 17
, Sarah A.: 28
EDINGTON, Easther J.: 24
EDMONDS, Jane: 48
ELLER, Frances: 46
ELLISON, Ellinor: 52
, Patsy: 10
ELMS, Mary Elizabeth: 68
, Nancy: 2
ELROAD, Mary: 65
ENGLAND, Amanda J.: 54
, Elcy: 67
, Elsy: 52
, Elizabeth: 3
, Jane: 5, 41
, Margaret: 39
, Mary H.: 36
, Pherebe: 68
, Rebecca: 3, 41, 56
EVANS, Charlotte: 40
, Eliza Jane: 62
, Mary E.: 8
, Melissa: 5
, Nancy M.: 59
, Somancey: 67
FANCHER, Amanda: 17
FARLEY, Elizabeth: 71
, Indianna: 51
, Jane: 71
, Lee Ann: 48
, Milly: 34
, Nancy: 9, 17, 32, 33
, Nancy Ann: 46
FARMINGTON, Mary M.: 71

-81-

FARRIS, Amaranda S.: 65
, Harriet: 53
, Mariah: 44
, Mary J.: 65
FELTON, Emaline: 73
, Ruthy: 30
FELTS: FELTZ
, Eliza: 72
, Elizabeth: 50
, Susan: 48
FIELDS, Sarah: 7
FINDLEY, Margarett: 19
FINNEY, Amanda E.: 14
FISHER, Nancy: 52
FISK: FISKE
, Ann: 12
, Lucinda: 33
FITCH, Sarahan: 63
FITE: Catharine: 65
FLINCHUM, Susannah: 35
FLINN: FLYNN
, Lona: 51
, Matilda: 15
, Nora: 51
, Rhoda: 55
FOSTER, Anny: 26
, Margaret: 3, 73
, Mary: 24
FOX, Jane: 26
, Malinda: 5
, Malitha: 25
, Martha: 25
, Mary T.: 70
, Nancy: 26
, Susan: 20
FRANKLIN, Mary Ann: 25
, Susan Jane: 35
FRANKS, Allisaria J.: 46
, Elizabeth: 63
, Nancy: 29
FRASIER: FRASUR: FRASURE
, Mrs. Agnes: 47
, Elizabeth Jane: 60
, Franky: 47
, Jane: 66
, Juda: 17
, Mary: 3(2), 15
, Sarah: 57
FROST, Elizabeth J.: 4
, Mary A.: 68
, Nancy A.: 30
, Rhody P.: 54

FRYER, Mary: 27
FRYES, Rose Anna: 10
GAMBLE, Elizabeth: 6
GARDNER, Elizabeth: 15
GAY, Elizabeth: 18
, Mary: 6
GEAR: GEER, Catharine: 12
, Martha: 24
, Mary L.: 72
, Polly Ann: 6
GENTRY, Alsy: 49
, Caroline: 16
GEORGE, Martha: 36
GERMAN, Betsy: 70
GIBBS, Hester C.: 39
, Mary: 10
, Mary E.: 39
GILL, Ellen: 16
GILLENTINE, Jane: 18
, Mary: 42
, Priscilla D.: 11, 55
GILLIALAND, Jane E.: 50
GIST, Martha: 68
, Mary: 69
, Rebecca: 68
, Sarah: 14
GLEESON, Eliza: 42
, Margaret: 27
, Mary: 59
GLENN, Eliza Jane: 60
, Elizabeth: 58
, Jane: 63
, Leann: 50
, Martha W.: 25
, Mary: 66
, Mary Ann: 63
, Nancy: 73
, Rachel: 45
, Sally Ann: 61
, Sarah: 2
, Sarah E.: 11
GLOVER, Sarah: 57
GOD(D)ARD, Elizabeth: 74
, Jane: 52
GOOCH, Jane: 11
, Lavina W.: 18
, Ra[c]hael: 58
GOOD, Polly Jane: 16
GOODBAR, Mary: 49
GOODWIN, Caroline E.: 2
, Louisa Ann: 72
, Mary: 32

GRAC(E)Y, Elizabeth A.: 36
, Jane: 36, 57
, Margaret: 58
, Mary: 67
, Nancy Y.: 57
, Sarah: 68
GRAG [GREGG?], Jane: 15
GRAHAM, Alevier: 26
, Ann: 68
, Elizabeth: 59, 61
, Leah: 62
, Margaret: 74
, Margaret Elvira: 50
, Mary: 55
, Mary Ana: 23
, Nancy Caroline: 10
, Nancy M. A. E.: 45
GRANT, Judith: 45
GRANTHAM, Charity: 27
, Jane: 15
, Sarah: 9
, Susan: 9
GRASTY, Margarett M.: 72
, Mary: 12
GRAVES, Adaliza: 62
, Ruth: 35
GRAY, Louisa Catherine: 31
GREEN(E), Amy Jane: 34
, Anna: 29
, Eliza Ann: 37
, Elizabeth: 3, 14
, Evaline: 2
, Mahulda: 4
, Martha: 34
, Martha J.: 1
, Mary: 58
, Mary J.: 63
, Nancy E.: 30
, Nancy J.: 9
, Rachael Emaline: 15
, Sarah: 19
, (Miss) Sarah: 73
, Sarah Griggs: 58
, Susan Jane: 24
, T. Attaline: 28
GREENFIELD, Elizabeth: 72
, Martha: 15
GREER, Cynthia: 61
, Elizabeth: 54
, Huldy: 30
, Lee Ann: 48
GREGG: See GRAG

GREGORY, Martha: 51
GRIFFIN, Susanna: 58
GRIFFITH, Martha: 58
, Martha L.: 65
, Nancy: 50
GRIME, Amey J.: 50
, Margaret E.: 13
GRISSOM, Mary: 25
GWINN, Frances: 10
HALE, Catharine P.: 37
, Malinda J.: 22
, Virginia: 18
HALTERMAN, Elizabeth: 40
, Mary: 40
HALY, Mary: 22
HAMBRICK: HEMBRICK
, Sarah: 23
, Wildy: 23
HAMBLETON: HAMILTON
, Martha: 48
, Mila: 31
, Susan: 74
HAMBLIN, Rheby: 74
HAMMONDS, Eliza: 8
HAMPTON, Eliza: 5
, Emeline: 68
HARBROUGH, Harriet: 32
HARDEN, Lucinda: 8
HARLOW, Margaret: 43
, Mary: 50
HARMON, Polly: 67
HARNESS, Diademy: 41
HARRIS, Hannah: 52
, Louisa D.: 56
, Margaret: 12
HARRISON, Emily: 29
, Naomi: 40
HART, Lucy Jane: 42
, Mary: 42
, Paralee: 12

HASTON: [also, HASTAIN, HASTINGS]
, Amanda: 15
, Malinda: 32
HATHAWAY, Eleanor Caroline: 37
, Mary A.: 43
HAWKINS, Matilda K.: 17
HAYNES, Sarah: 67
HAYSE, Sarah: 10
HEARN, Birdy: 45
HEIFNER: HEFNER, Nancy: 29
, Luzana: 2

HENCLEY: HENSELEY: HENSLY
, Elizabeth: 71
, Elizabeth C.: 22
, Nancy: 28
HENDERSON, Elizabeth: 46
, Mahala: 40
, (Miss) Mary: 71
HEN(N)ESSEE, Alcy: 64
, Catherine: 8
, Mary: 62
HENR(E)Y, Anney: 71
, Aryella: 33
, Catharine: 6
, Clarissa: 46
, Clementine H.: 12
, Cynthiann: 56
, Dicey: 12
, Eliza Jane: 64
, Elizabeth: 19
, Jane: 8
, Juliann: 51
, Loranny: 27
, Lucy: 55
, Nancy: 70
, Rebecca: 8
, Rosa: 5
HENSEY, Jane: 8
HERBERT, Polly: 55
HERD, Ann Jane: 9
, Elizabeth: 46
, Martha: 37
, Nancy: 60
, Sarah: 30, 55
, Susan: 70
, Susannah: 68
HICKEY, Ann Eliza: 41
, Elizabeth: 48
, Mary: 39
, Saraphina C.: 21
, Sophronia: 8
HICKMAN, Judith Ann: 20
HILL, Cynthia C.: 27
, Elizabeth: 66
, Laniza: 45
, Louisa: 74
, Mrs. Margaret: 8
, Martha J.: 54
, Mary: 48
, Matilda: 20
, Susan D.: 54
, Susannah: 29
HITCHCOCK, Ann: 26

HITCHCOCK, Malinda: 66
, Malinda C.: 45
, Mary: 19
, Mary Ann: 31
, Polly: 11
, Susan: 5
HODGE(S), Jane: 40
, Malvina: 43
, Nancy: 9
, Nancy C.: 59
HOLDER, Brittania: 34
, Caroline: 36
, Eliza: 23
, Elizabeth: 17, 31
, Jane: 31
, Margaret: 62
, Martha: 23
, Mary: 28, 37
, Mary Ann: 8
, Nancy: 5
, S. Adaline: 62
, Sarah: 65
, Tabitha: 20
HOLDERFIELD, Fanny: 58
, Louisa: 24
HOLLAND, Elizabeth: 57
, Elizabeth Ann: 34
, Martha: 31
, Mary R.: 57
, Melrainy: 56
, Nancy: 69
, Prissee: 49
, Rebecca: 49
, Sarah E.: 30
HOLLANDSWORTH: HOLLINSWORTH
, Lucy: 39, 61
HOL(E)MAN, Frances: 72
, Julia Ann Olly La-
titia: 14
, Malinda: 23
, Margrett: 53
, Polly: 33
, Susannah: 54
HOLMES, Maniza: 30
, Nancy: 61
HOOPER, Caroline: 44
, Dosea E.: 40
, Mary: 39
, Susannah: 19
HOOTEN, Jane: 11
HOPKINS, Catherine: 57
HORSLY, Margaret: 67

HOWARD, Aralissa: 71
, Charlotta: 31
, Eliza: 62
, Elizabeth M.: 21
, Hulda: 20
, Judith: 10
, Levicey: 3
, Louisa: 30
, Lucinda: 72
, Martha: 68
, Mary: 11, 19, 23, 36
, Matilda: 26, 67
, Myra: 26
, Rebecca: 4
, Sarah: 34
, Zealy D.: 63
HOWEL(L), Agatha: 1
, Elizabeth: 10
, Lucinda: 9
, Lucy Jane: 30
, Selia: 37
, Senith: 20
HUDDLESTON, Margarett P.: 49
, Rebecca: 59
HUDGENS, Amanda: 8
, Catharine: 42
, Nancy: 29
HUGHS, Rachel: 30
HUNTER, Angeline E.: 32
, Anna Narcissa: 30
, Bethia: 12
, Elizabeth: 29, 42
, Henrietta: 42
, Jane: 61
, Mary: 61, 67 (2)
, Mary A.: 31
, Mary Louisa: 42
, Minerva: 40
, Sarah: 33
, Zilly: 64
HURT, Mary: 42
HUTCHIN(G)S, Amarinda: 34
, Ann: 20
, Anna: 38
, Jane: 34
, Kiza: 41
, Lecrease: 60
, Mary: 17, 20
, Nancy: 41
, Sarah: 55
, Sarah H.: 34
, Stacey: 39

HUTSON, Creacy: 47
, Eleanor W.: 14
, Julia Ann: 22
, Louvinia: 64
, Martha: 50
, Mary Jane: 40
, Sarah: 5, 22, 46
, Susan: 22
HYDER, Catharine: 32
, Lavina: 33
INGALLS, Martha L.: 1
IRWIN, Ellen D.: 35
, Margaret A.: 25
, Margaret J.: 45
, Rebecca T.: 28
ISHAM: IS(S)OM
, Elizabeth: 21
, Mary: 6
, Silah: 19
JACKSON, Catherine: 64
, Elizabeth: 2
, Mareagett: 54
, Nancy: 66
, Sarah: 55
, Susan: 64
JACOBS, Absley: 73
, Leale Elizabeth: 29
, Letha: 65
JAMES, Elizabeth: 26, 28
, Martha J.: 53
JANUARY, Elizabeth: 26
JARNAGIN, Zilpha W. J.: 34
JARVIS, Mary: 10, 63
, Meekey Ann: 44
JAY, Minerva: 62
JENKINS, Louisa: 4
, Mary E.: 17
JETT, Eliza: 53
, Sarah: 24
JOHNSON, Jane: 32
, Nancy: 34
, Tempa: 6
JOHNSTON, Mary: 49
, Mary N.: 74
JONES, Amanda: 26
, Ann: 70
, Catharine: 7
, Celina: 26
, Elinder: 67
, Eliza: 10, 57
, Elizabeth: 60, 75
, Elizabeth E.: 5

JONES, Margaret: 16
 , Martha Ann: 26
 , Mary Jane: 16, 30
 , Nancy: 8
 , Nancy Ann: 60
 , Polleymena: 57
 , Samira: 75
 , Sarah: 49
 , Sufiney C.: 60
JORDON, Sarah: 52
JULI(E)N, America: 71
 , Amerilla: 12
KATHCART, Phebe: 10
KEATHLEY: KEATHLY: KEITHLEY
 , Amanda C.: 13
 , Catharine: 1
 , Eliza Ann: 65
 , Louisa: 30
 , Lucinda: 13
 , Mary: 15
 , Mary Jane: 65
 , Pernetta C.: 13
 , Sarah: 66
 , Susan: 48
KELLY, Mary: 29
KERBY: KIRBY
 , Mahaly J.: 23
 , Margaret: 46
 , Mary: 64
 , Milly: 38
 , Nancy: 53
 , Susan: 73
KERR, Eliza: 29
 , Lucy C.: 4
 , Martha J.: 1
KETCHERSIDE, Trimanda M. C.: 51
KIDWELL, Angeletta: 46
 , Janetta: 40
KIN, Rebecca: 7
KING, Nancy: 69
KINNARD, Jane: 6
KIRK(E), Lucy Ann: 16
 , Martha: 37
 , Nancy: 38, 61
 , Susan: 35
KITTRELL, Nancy Ann: 3
KNOWLES, Elizabeth: 34
 , Jane: 35, 65
 , Mahala: 33
 , Martha: 14
 , Nancy F.: 27
 , Polly: 11

KNOWLES, Rachael: 33
KUHN, Jane: 4
KYLE, Peggy: 16
LAFEVER(S), America: 49
 , Celia: 32
 , Nancy: 31
LAMB, Maria: 61
LANCE, Mary E.: 33
 , Rose Ann: 42
 , Sarah: 50
LANDRUN, Patience: 14
LANE, Mrs. Mary A.: 7
LASKINS, Elizabeth: 15
LAVENDER, Cynthia L.: 28
LAY, Nancy: 29
 , Sarah: 56
LEDBETTER, Tempy L. M.: 22
LEE, Abigail: 37
 , Lavina R.: 19
 , Rachel: 62
 , Ruth: 28
 , Susannah: 53
LEFTWICH, Emily C.: 60
 , (Miss) Louisa: 61
 , Mary E.: 17
 , Matilda J.: 11
LEWIS, Caroline V.: 12
 , Clementine: 47
 , Eliza B.: 74
 , Emily: 69
 , Jane: 6
 , Manerva: 23
 , Martha: 18, 71
 , Martha E.: 39
 , Mary: 47
 , Matilda: 43
 , Nancy: 41
 , Sarah: 41, 44
 , Temperence: 56
LINCOLN, Jane: 47
LINVILLE, Margaret: 3
LISK, Luraney C.: 40
 , Mary L.: 47
LITTLE, Aneliza: 21
 , Charlotte: 2
 , Harriet Jane: 69
 , Laminda P.: 27
 , Lotty: 26
 , Mahala J.: 35
 , Mary: 31
 , Mary Emily: 24
 , Mary M. T.: 37

LITTLE, Nancy A.: 2
, Rebecca: 60
, Sarah D.: 11
LOLLAR, Arey L.: 33
, Elizabeth: 52
, Henrietta: 36
, Martha: 38
, Mary: 33
, Mary Jane: 1
, Rebecca: 38
LONG, Manerva: 44
LOWELL, Elizabeth S.: 26
, Harriett Jane: 26
, Hester Ann: 53
, Sarah E. M.: 63
LOWERY: LOWREY: LOWRY
, Amey: 33
, Caroline: 4
, Elizabeth: 12
, Emaline: 73
, Margarett: 28
, Mary E.: 31
, Paulina: 73
, Sarah: 33
LONDEY: LUNDY
, Christiana: 58
, Elizabeth: 8
, Rhoda: 32
, Sarah: 58
LYDA, Diana: 46
, Louisa: 6
, Rhody: 53
, Sarah: 6
McBRIDE, Leann: 69
, Lydia Margaret: 59
, Mahala: 2
, Mary: 39
, Nancy: 61
, Susannah: 21
McCAIN, Malinda: 19
McCANCE, Martha Jane: 10
McCLAIN, Polly: 68
McCLUIN, Lucinda: 48
McCONNEL(L), Eliza: 62
, Elizabeth: 36
, Esther J.: 60
, Harriett: 7
, Louisa: 11
, Myra: 32
, Nancy: 60
McCORMICK, Elizabeth: 6
, Mary Ann: 56

McCORMICK, Marylene: 27
, Sarah: 59
McCOY, Mary: 63
McCRORY, Sarah Ann: 62
McCULLOUGH, Elizabeth: 45
McCULLY, Oma: 69
McDANIEL, Martha: 59
, Mary: 3
, Mary Ann: 12
McELROY, Martha: 73
McEWIN, Arreny: 63
, Elizabeth: 35
McGARR, Elizabeth: 13
, Sarah Ann: 13
McGHEE, Elizabeth: 10
McGOWAN: McGOWN
, Desa: 57
, Keziah: 12
, Nancy: 31
, Roxy Ann: 29
McGUIRE, Lavinnia: 8
McMATH, Nancy: 45
, Rebecca: 59
McMANUS, Mary E.: 21
McPHEARSON: McPHERSON
, Clarinda: 71
, Nancy: 8
McVILANIE, Lydia F.: 14
MALDEN: MAULDEN
, Jane: 53
, Louisa: 67
MANES, Polly Ann: 73
MANNING, Elizabeth: 44
, Judia: 44
, Sarah: 28
MANOS, Vina: 55
MARCUM: MARKUM
, Lydia: 26
, Mary: 24
, Rachel: 53
MARLOW, Malinda: 71
MARR: MARRS: MARS
, Leacy: 73
, Louisa: 69
, Sarah: 36
MARTIN, Elizabeth: 70
, Malinda: 66
, Maria L.: 36
, Rilda: 43
MASON, Amanda: 22
, Elizabeth Jane: 30
, Lacy: 28

MASON, Margaret(t): 7, 72
    , Mary: 43
    , Nancy: 51
    , Sookey: 58
MASSA, Charlotte: 48
    , Elizabeth: 65
    , Marinda Caroline: 55
    , Mary: 55
MATLOCK, Evaline: 13
    , Mary Ann: 9
MATTHEWS, Elender: 20
MATTOCK, Jane: 41
MAY, Martha E.: 70
MAYBERRY, Mary: 71
MAYNOR, Sarah Jane: 50
MAYSE, Christiana J.: 52
MEDCALF: METCALF
    , Lucinda: 72
    , Jelina: 33
MEEK, Amanda: 42
    , Elizabeth: 13, 15
    , Emily E.: 9
    , Marion: 49
MENIS, Letitia: 65
MANEFEE: MENNEFEE: MENNIFEE
    , Cynthia B.: 13
    , Roda J.: 27
    , Susan: 46
MERCER, Angeletty: 51
MEREDITH, Jane: 37
    , Martha: 28
MIDGET, Pauline: 10
MILAM, Jane: 13
    , Sarah: 3
MILICAN, Margaret O.: 4
MILLER, Elizabeth: 41
    , Emaline: 47
    , Emily E.: 8
    , Frances: 47
    , Hannah: 38
    , Jemima: 23
    , Manerva: 59
    , Nancy: 23
    , Nelley: 72
    , Parilee: 43
    , Susan A.: 45
MILLS, Elizabeth J.: 52
    , Mary: 4
    , Mary M.: 54
MILLSAP(S), Martha: 61
    , Rosanna: 51
MILLYETTE, Jane: 46

MITCHELL, Adaline: 19
    , Drusilla: 22
    , Edith: 67
    , Feraby: 59
    , Frances: 37
    , Isabella: 57
    , Malvina: 35
    , Martha: 49
    , Martha Ann: 16
    , Martha J.: 8
    , Mary: 11
    , Mary R.: 57
    , Mira J.: 74
    , Nancy: 14, 65, 70
    , Rachel: 14, 68
    , Sarah: 43
    , Sophia: 28
MONTGOMERY, Sally: 13
MOON, Ariselar: 50
MOONEYHAM, Sally: 23, 59
MOORE, Arminda: 34
    , Elenor: 51
    , Elizabeth: 1, 43
    , Fanny: 26
    , Frances: 12
    , Leitha Jane: 66
    , Malissa: 56
    , Manerva: 69
    , Mary: 51
    , Minerva: 57
    , Nancy: 25, 61
    , Permelia A.: 14
    , Rebecca: 50
    , Tabitha: 65
MORGAN, Jamima: 53
    , Juliann M.: 42
MORRIS, Sarah Ann: 28
    , Sophah: 17
MORRISON, Rebecca: 50
MORROW, Ruth Elizabeth: 68
MOSS, Nancy: 24
    , Sarah: 54
    , Tabitha: 5
NASH, Delila: 10
NEMORE, Sally: 49
NERO, Martha Susannah: 43
NETHERTON, Eliza Jane: 1
    , Mary: 24
    , Rhody: 29
NEWMAN, Mary C.: 48
NICHOLAS, Elizabeth: 32
NICHOLS, Elizabeth: 31

NICHOLS, Pressia Ann: 59
NOLAND: NOLEN, Demercius: 58
, Elizabeth: 20
, Emaline: 7
NORRIS, Rachel: 25
, Sarah: 45
, Tabitha: 44
ODLE, Priscilla: 24
, Sarah: 14
OFFICER, Altazarle W.: 69
, Amand C.: 62
, Catherine P.: 69
, Margaret C.: 47
, Susannah: 21
OGDEN, Mary: 32
OLIVER, Nancy: 34
OVERBEE, Elizabeth: 57
OWENS: OWING
, Nancy: 60
, Sarah: 20
OXFORD, Armina: 63
PARKER, Elizabeth: 29
, Mary Jane: 63
, Polly: 38
PARKS, Jane: 13
, Mary: 19
, Susanah: 8
PARISH, Frances: 53
, Mary: 26
PASS, (Miss) Ann J.: 47
, Ann Johnson: 16
, Catherine: 71
PASSONS, Amanda: 69
, Helen A.: 43
PATILLAR, Nancy Caroline: 42
PATRICK, Polly Ann: 54
PATTERSON, Amanda: 7
PATTON, Mary: 61
, Matilda: 65
, Nancy: 54
, Sarah Ann: 13
PAULSTON, Susan: 37
PAYNE, Lucretia: 22
, Lydia: 31
, Margaret: 21
PAIN, Matilda: 47
PEARIN, Jane: 57
PEARSON, Ann: 38
, Mary Ann: 18
, Sarah: 37
PENNINGTON, Altemira: 68
, Elizabeth: 17

PENNINGTON, Jane: 14
, Roda Ann: 68
PERKINS, Dicy R.: 71
, Michel: 59
PETTIT, Deniza: 22
, Nancy: 15
PHILLIPS, Nancy: 15
, Sarah: 45
, Tabitha B.: 47
PHY, Eliza Ann: 53
, Peggy: 9
PINEGAR, Susannah: 50
PINNER, Mrs. Elizabeth: 30
, Mrs. Jane: 32
PIRTLE, Lucinda: 52
, Margaret J.: 35
, Mary Ann: 73
, Susan: 2
PLUMMER, Josephine: 54
POE, Mary Jane: 19
POGUE, Lydia: 31
POLLARD, Elizabeth A.: 31
, Emily S. A.: 52
, Louisa: 64
, Rachel: 19
POPE, Frances: 28 (2)
, Jane: 39
POTEET, Christiana: 9
POTTS, Catharine: 16
, Susan: 47
PRATER: PRATOR: [PRATHER]
, Amanda: 18
, Arleave: 28
, Elizabeth: 18
, Susan: 17
PRESLEY, Ann: 74
PRICE, Elizabeth: 28
, Elizabeth E.: 36
, Fanny: 57
, (Miss) Jane: 25
, Margaret J.: 5
PRINCE, Manerva: 69
PROCK, Dorcas: 42
PROVINCE, Judea: 17
QUARLES, Delilah: 42
, Matilda: 59
, Sarah: 74
QUILLEN, Eliza: 39
, Zeda: 1
RAMSEY, Jane: 68
, Margaret: 54
, Martha: 12

RAMSEY, Mary Ann: 56
, Sarah: 74
RANDALS, Amanda: 63
, Arthusa: 27
, Hasty: 6
, Lucinda: 67
RANDOLPH, Lucilla: 12
, Manerva: 54
, Patience: 64
RASCOE, Ammalise: 39
, Martha Ann: 39
RAWLINGS, Mary: 32
RHEA, Catharine: 12
, Elizabeth J.: 41
, Sarah: 41
RICE, Elizabeth: 22
, Elvira: 23
, Matilda C.: 33
RICHT, Mary: 18
RICKMAN, Jane: 56
, Mary Jane: 19
, Polly: 13
RICKS, Cornelia: 19
, Martha Ann: 19
RIDGE, Nancy: 26
RIGSBY, Patsy: 27
, Sally: 20
ROACH, Jane: 51
, Martha Ann: 43
ROBBINS, Elizabeth: 7
, Margaret E.: 50
, Mary J.: 2
, Martely: 44
, Nancy Ann Jane: 53
, Paulina L. J.: 34
ROBERSON, Ann: 38
, Elizabeth Evaline: 20
, Wincy: 29
, Elvira: 5
ROBERTS, Catherine: 39
, Elizabeth Jane: 22
, Lucinda: 55
, Mary: 57
, Mary Ann: 44
, Milly: 36
, Paulina: 6
, Phebe: 56
, Rutha: 64
, Sarah E.: 66
, Susan: 15, 68
, Susannah: 47
ROBINSON, Arzella: 4

ROBINSON, Louisa: 74
, Margaret C.: 24
, Rebecca: 16, 35
ROBISON, Martha: 64
, Sarah: 60
ROCHHOLD, Margaret J.: 5
RODGERS: ROGERS
, Blanchey: 10
, Elizabeth: 10
, Elizabeth M.: 57, 67
, Hulda R.: 19
, Lucinda: 50
, Malinda: 24
, Mary: 5
, Mary A.: 40
, Mary Jane: 56
, Mary M.: 15
, Matilda: 69
, Nancy V.: 5
, Polly Ann: 41
, Sarah: 70
, Susan Jane: 51
ROSE, Susan: 44
ROSLIR, Adline: 24
ROSS, Eliza Jane: 45
, Rachael: 51
ROWLAND, Jane: 41
, Lucy Ann: 58
, Malinda: 12
ROYAL, Sarah L.: 63
RUSSELL, Caroline: 68
RUTLEDGE, Susan Jane: 23
SAILORS: SAYLORS
, Elizabeth: 61
, Nancy Jane: 4
, Sarah: 44
, Sarah A.: 12
SAPP, Nancy: 58
SAUNDERS, Elizabeth: 6
SAVAGE, Elizabeth: 35
, Jane: 24
, Mary: 11, 33
, Sarah: 52
SAYERS, Margaret: 51
SCARBOROUGH: SCARBROUGH
, Agnes: 33
, Lucy J.: 61
, Margaret Ann: 6
, Susan M.: 16
SCOGGIN(S), Amy: 72
, Celia: 43
, Matilda: 4

SCOGGIN(S), (Miss) Mary: 40
, Sarah: 45
SCOTT, Delina S.: 14
, Helen: 22
, Mary Jane: 50
, Minerva J.: 16
, Nancy Priscilla: 58
, Sarah: 69
SCURLOCK, Martha: 44
, Nancy: 26
SELF, Temperence: 22
SERVEL, Mary: 29
SEVIER, Mary Ann: 28
SEWELL, Nancy: 72
SHANNON, Artamissa: 41
SHAW, Frances M.: 45
, Teresa: 48
SHERRELL: SHERRILL
, Ann: 33
, Linney: 38
, Margarett E.: 31
, Maria Jane: 44
SHOCKLEY, Ruth: 73
SHORT, Maximilla: 44
, Nancy: 2, 40
, Rhoda: 49
, Sarah: 26, 36
, Sntha: 53
SHUSTER, Caroline: 39
, Louisa A.: 66
SIMMONS, Elizabeth M.: 3
, Stacy: 55
SIMPSON, Evaline: 47
, Jane M.: 26
, Margaretta B.: 73
, Polly: 41
, Sally: 56
SIMRIL, Maranda: 35
, Parasetta: 29
SIMS, Clarissa J.: 14
, Helen L.: 65
, Sarah: 13
SINGLETON, Susan: 7
SLATTEN, Eliza J.: 53
, Martha: 17
SLUDER, Rebecca: 70
SLYGER, Martha A.: 70
SMITH, Almeady: 37
, Cynthia M.: 30
, Easther: 50
, Elizabeth: 1
, Frances Jane: 48

SMITH, Jane: 18, 48, 70
, Martha Ann: 3
, Mary E.: 30
, Nancy: 35, 55
, Pernetta: 15
, Sally: 23
, Sarah: 4
, Tymanda: 38
SNIDER, Martha: 51
SNODGRASS, Eliza Ann: 42
, Eliza J.: 22
, Elizabeth: 55
, Emily: 50
, Martha: 52
, Martha P.: 41
, Mary: 13
, Mary Ann: 50
SORELL, Catharine M.: 27
SOUTHARD, Josephine: 66
, Louisa: 38
, Matilda Caroline: 43
, Susan Matilda: 32
SPARKMAN, Amanda: 16, 69
, Eady: 36
, Margaret: 60
, Mary: 16
, Sally Ann: 53
SPARKS, Mary: 62
, Phebe: 58
SPECK, Mary: 29
SPEERS, Jane: 31
SPERRY, Elizabeth: 8
, Sarah A.: 24
SPUR(R), Juliana: 11
, Sarah: 28
STACEY: STACY
, Cynthia J.: 18
, Elizabeth: 63
, Rebecca: 3
STAMPS, Elizabeth: 29
, Unity: 59
STANLEY, Elizabeth: 57
STEEL(E), Dorcas: 49
, Julia A.: 11
STEPHENS, Jarusha: 32
STEWART, Agness: 23, 49
, Elizabeth: 40
, Julia: 28
, Malvina C.: 39
, Margaret Amanda: 51
, Mary: 53
, Mary Bersheba: 19

STEWART: STWART
  , Nancy: 26, 34
  , Nancy F.: 7
  , Rachel D.: 35
  , Sarah: 63
  , Sian: 25
STILES, Margaret Ann: 37
  , Mary Elizabeth: 37
STINETT, Louisa: 53
STOCKTON, Martha Jane: 25
STREET, Frances: 17
SUTTLE, Elizabeth: 29
  , Jane: 4
  , Susannah: 12
  , Wincy: 8
SWEAT, Julia Ann: 14
SWIFT, Hellen: 71
SWINDLE, Anna: 39
  , Diana: 55
  , Isabel: 56
  , Sarah: 16, 35
  , Susan: 44, 72
TABER, Mary: 65
TACKET, Mary: 16
TALLENT, Jane: 5
  , Sarah: 67
TANNER, Martha: 68
TATE, Elizabeth: 72
TAYLOR, Ann E.: 3, 54
  , Caroline: 64
  , Charlotta: 2
  , Eleanor: 5
  , Eliza: 22
  , Elizabeth: 20
  , Lorina S.: 35
  , Louisa: 15
  , Margaret: 70
  , Martha: 38
  , Martha A.: 21
  , Martha J.: 42
  , Mary: 44
  , Mary C.: 32
  , Mary E.: 34
  , Mary Jane: 55
  , Sarah Jane: 69
TEATERS: TEETERS
  , Nancy: 41
  , Susan: 25
TEMPLETON, Amanda: 61
  , Eliza: 11
  , Nancy: 72
  , Narcissa S.: 60

THOMAS, Alcey: 33
  , Jane: 46
  , Mahaly: 6
  , Maria Lucy: 70
  , Sarah: 46, 48
  , Sarah Ann: 67
THOMPSON, Rebecca: 18
TINDLE, Mary Ann: 19
TITTLETON, Jane: 21
TODD, Mary Ann: 3
TOLISON, Charlotte: 4
  , Sarah: 4
TOMBOLIN, Celia: 73
TRAUBOUGH: TROBAUGH
  , Rachel: 39
  , Sarah Ann: 39
TRUETT, Margarett: 1
TUCKER, Eliza: 13
  , Harriet J.: 61
  , Luncinda: 24
  , Matilda: 15
  , Mary: 23
  , Ruth B.: 52
  , Sarah: 56
TURNER, Anna: 46
  , Eliza: 67
  , Elizabeth: 36, 66
TURNEY, Lucinda F.: 70
UNDERWOOD, Eliza: 74
  , Emily Manerva: 29
  , Mary: 30
  , Sarah: 56
UPCHURCH, Minerva: 63
  , Nancy J.: 53
USREY: USSERY
  , Elizabeth A.: 67
  , Tennessee: 13
  , Lucy R.: 11
VASS, Ann: 49
  , Betty: 36
  , Mary F.: 13
VAUGN, Heilen: 45
VEST, Jane: 73

WADDLE, Delila: 52
  , Nigary Ann: 15
WALKER, Elizabeth W.: 27
  , Lucinda: 46
  , Martha Ann: 48
  , Mary: 21
  , Mary Jane: 28
  , Nancy Jane: 14

WALLACE: WALLIS
  , Alzira: 18
  , Delilea: 70
  , Mahala: 9
  , Malinda: 60
  , Martha: 64
  , Mary: 21
  , Mary H.: 42
  , Matilda: 75
  , Mrs. Rachel: 41
  , Sarah: 4, 41
WALLER, Eliza: 33
WALLING, Eliza: 50, 75
  , Mary: 12, 57, 74
  , Nancy: 7
  , Phebe: 25
  , Pheby: 30
  , Phebe Ann: 14
  , Ruth: 25
  , Sarah: 12
  , Susan: 69
  , Susannah: 27
WARD, Almyra: 7(2)
WARNER, Elizabeth: 20
  , Lewiza: 8
WARREN, Agness: 39
  , Elizabeth: 48
  , Julia: 10
  , Mary E.: 3
  , Sarah A.: 74
WATERS, Susan: 65
WATSON, Elizabeth G.: 64
  , Harriet L.: 45
  , Keziah Martha: 49
  , Maria A.: 65
  , Mary Ann: 1
WEATHERFORD: WETHERFORD
  , Jane: 21
  , Martha: 21
  , Rosa: 53
WEAVER, Caroline: 2
  , Eliza: 60
  , Elizabeth: 37
  , Frances E. J.: 55
  , Leann: 64
  , Margaret: 8
  , Matilda Jane: 20
  , Nancy J.: 43
  , Omey: 21
  , Polly: 36
  , Sarah: 25
  , Sarah Angeline: 64

WEBB, Jane: 44
  , Martha Ann: 24
  , Melissa: 5
  , Nancy Jane: 69
  , Sarah: 37
WEBSTER, Elizabeth: 24, 63
  , Sarah: 38
WELCH, Jane: 2
  , Nancy: 23
WESSON, Julia: 65
WHEELER, Pharda Malinda C.: 58
WHITACRE: WHITAKER: WHITEAKER
  , Hannah: 9
  , Margaret: 70
  , Nancy: 60
  , Rebecca: 46
  , Sarah: 46, 70
WHITE, Catharine Elvira: 4
  , Dicy P.: 68
  , (Miss) Fanny: 9
  , Louisa Hurt: 27
  , Louisa Jane: 7
  , Margaret: 51
  , Martha: 37, 49
  , Maria: 42
  , Mary: 2, 70
  , Milly Ann: 33
  , Nancy: 5
  , Sally: 9
  , Sarah C.: 13
WHITFIELD, Mary Ann: 30
WHITLEY, Hetty: 70
  , Letitia: 24
  , Lucinda Jane: 2
  , Nancy: 2
WHITMORE, Mary Elizabeth: 4
WHITSON, Dolly: 6
  , Martha J.: 71
  , Mary: 6
  , Mary Jane: 22
  , Nancy: 35
  , Sarah: 32(2)
WHITTLEY, Mary L.: 24
WIGGINS, Serona: 35
WIL(L)HITE, Elizabeth: 21
  , Janetta: 21
  , Jennetta B.: 40
  , Mary Ann: 4
  , Mary J.: 48
  , Nancy: 33
  , Polly Ann: 12
  , Senora J.: 57

WILLIAMS, Abigail: 40
       , Elizabeth: 22, 28, 60
       , Leann: 24
       , Malvina: 20
       , Mary: 32
       , Sarah: 6
WILLIAMSON, Lydia Caroline: 27
WIL(L)SON, Amanda: 43
       , Barthena: 66
       , Eliza E.: 64
       , Elizabeth: 18
       , Jane: 13
       , Lamira: 4
       , Martha Jane: 1
       , Nancy: 48
       , Sarah: 52
       , Sarah Emeline: 58
WINSTEAD, Margaret: 52
WISDOM, Clementine B. H.: 30
       , Elizabeth: 42
       , Jane: 36
       , Julian: 71
       , Mrs. Sarah: 9
       , Telitha: 16
WITT, Dysey: 23
       , Hannah G.: 16, 62
WOMACK, Lucinda: 43
       , Mary: 68
       , Mary Jane: 56

WOMICK, Nancy: 16
WOOD, Elizabeth: 47
WOODSON, Frances E.: 25
WORLEY, Agness: 38
       , Creda: 74
       , Emaline J.: 47
       , Lila: 54
       , Lucretia: 74
       , Martha: 42, 67
       , Nancy: 74
       , Rebecca Ann: 3
       , Sarah: 74
WRIGHT, Margaret: 22
WYCOFF, Rachel Elvira: 15
YATES, Nancy: 63
       , Sarah: 18
YEAGER, Camelian: 51
       , Eglantine S.: 7
       , Eliza M.: 73
       , Liza Ann: 47
       , Phebe Emaline: 73
YEATS, Elizabeth: 56
YOUNG, A. Leathy: 58
       , Marian L.: 58
       , Martha: 67
       , Mary: 25
       , Patsy: 75
       , Sarah: 72
       , Sophronia: 25

GENERAL INDEX TO:
MINISTERS, J. P's. (the latter usually designated as "Esquire"),
and all other persons mentioned in the text, aside from the contracting parties,
with miscellaneous notes on some of the ministers.

_____, Rev. Wm.: 68
ANDERSON, Rev. Isaac:["The Rev. Isaac
  Anderson and others will preach at
  the courthouse in Sparta, on the
  4th Sabbath in this month." Sparta
  Review, Wednesday, Oct. 13, 1824.]
ANDERSON, Martha: 40
ANDERSON, Wm. M., Esq.: 6, 22, 44
ANDERSON, Rev. Zachariah: 17, 18, 23.
  [Two-Seed-In-The-Spirit Baptist.]
ARNOLD, Hayes(se), Esq.: 42, 48, 52,
  61, 70
AUSTIN, Wm., Esq.: 3, 13, 44, 45, 51,
  52, 67, 68, 72
AVERY, John H[enry]: 3. ["A Fragmen-
  tary Genealogical Record of the
  Descendants of Myer Avery and his
  son Peter Avery", p. 7.]
BAPTIST CHURCH, CONCORD. See: Rev.
  Isaac Denton, Jr., below.
BAPTIST CHURCH, STONE'S SEMINARY-Free
  Will. See: Rev. Thomas Stone
BARR, Rev. Wm.: 60
BARTLETT, Jas., Esq.: 6, 9, 70
BENNETT, Leonidas H., Esq. (also, Rev.):
  6, 13, 38, 39, 44, 51, 59, 64
BENNETT, Walker: 37
BENNETT, Wm. H.: 45
BOONE, Daniel: 33
BOUNDS, Wm. C., Esq.: 7, 9, 44, 51, 64
BOYD, Rev. Wm.: 73
BRADFORD, W. K., Esq.: 21, 52
BRADL(E)Y, Richard, Esq.: 1, 4, 7, 8,
  10, 14, 23, 40, 46, 49, 50, 54, 56,
  61, 67, 68, 72
BROCKETT, Rev. M. Y.(N.?): 3, 8, 9, 10,
  12, 15, 18, 19, 20, 21, 22, 24, 25,
  28, 35, 39, 40, 42, 45, 47, 48, 51,
  57, 58, 59, 62, 63, 66, 67. [Pres-
  byterian.]
BRUSTER, Wm., Esq.: 23
BROWN, Rev. J. L.: 37
BROWN, Rev. S. H.:[He was appointed to
  the pastorate of the Sparta Meth-
  odist church in 1858, where he remained one year.]
BROWN, Tilman, Esq.: 15, 48

BROYLES, Hosea. See: Rev. W. C. Haislip
BRYAN(T), James H.: iii, 63
BRYAN, John, Esq.: 3, 7, 9, 50
BRYAN, Wm.: 3
BUCK, Isaac, Esq.: 9, 45, 56, 66
BURDEN, Rev. Wm.: 4, 6, 9, 18, 23, 24,
  26, 31, 43, 50, 51, 53, 61, 63, 72,
  73. [Methodist.]
BURUM, Nancy. See: Rev. Peter Burum
BURU(E)M, Rev. Peter: 29, 45, 53. [He
  m. Nancy Burum, Dec. 11, 1853. In
  Oct., 1858, Nancy Burum made will
  which gave freedom to her slave, who
  was to be sent to the west coast of
  Africa. The will was probated Nov.
  1867, White Co. Will Book 1860-72,
  p. 20. Peter Burum is buried at Mt.
  Pisgah Methodist Church. His tomb-
  stone: "Born Oct. 27, ___; Died
  Sept. 21, 1856".]
BUSSELL, Alvey [Alva?], Esq.: 2, 3, 4,
  5, 11, 13, 20, 21, 22, 37, 43, 45,
  46, 48, 49, 60, 61, 64, 65, 67
BUXTON, Rev. Stephen G.: 17, 35, 37, 38,
  39, 52, 55
CAMERON, Elisha, Esq.: 56, 57, 62, 71
CAMP, Wm. E., Esq.: 29, 42, 55, 59, 66
CARNES, Rev. Wm. D.: 61, 70
CERTAIN, Asa, Esq.: 3, 5, 13, 17, 18,
  23, 28, 29, 34, 35, 38, 57, 67
CHISUM, Mr. ____: v
CHURCH OF CHRIST, LANSDEN. See: Rev.
  James K. Lansden
CITY CEMETERY. See: Rev. Wm. Jared
CLARK, Isaac: 15
CLARK, Jesse B., Esq.: 8, 50
CLARK, Joseph W., Esq.: 2, 12
CLAYTON, Wm., Esq.: 2, 3, 4, 7, 8, 9,
  10, 13, 14, 15, 16, 17, 19, 20, 21,
  24, 28, 30, 32, 37, 38, 40, 42, 47,
  48, 49, 57, 65, 67, 73, 74
COLE, Rev. Jesse: 16, 20, 31, 39, 60
COOPER, Alexander: 54. [Revol. soldier.]
COOPER, Thos., Esq.: 5, 24, 57, 67
COPELAND, Rev. A. G.: 22. [He was list-
  ed in Dist. No. 2, 1850 Census for
  White Co., as "Minister of the Gos-

pel M.E." Born in Tenn., 1826, probably son of James W. & Margaret Copeland.]

COPELAND, James W. See: Rev. A. G., immediately above.

COPELAND, Margaret (___). See: Rev. A. G., above.

CORBIN, Rev. ___. [He was appointed to the pastorate of the Sparta Methodist congregation in 1856 and apparently left in 1857.]

COULSON, Rev. David: 13, 70

CROOK, John, Esq.: 2, 6, 19, 20, 21, 24, 30, 51, 54, 55, 60, 61, 62, 63, 65, 68

CROWDER, Richard, Esq.: 16, 17, 44, 51, 64

CUMMINGS, Joseph, J.P.: 69

DALE, John: 18. [Revolutionary soldier]

DEARING, Sims, Esq.: 6, 12, 28, 43, 47, 54

DEFREES, Geo., Esq.: 8, 27, 28, 38, 53, 61, 71

DEITZ, Rev. Aaron: 4, 55

DENTON, Elijah W., Esq.: 1, 8, 12, 14, 17, 22, 23, 29, 36, 41, 43, 46, 48, 54, 62, 65, 66, 69, 73, 74

DENTON, Rev. Isaac, Sr. See: Rev. Isaac Jr., below.

DENTON, Rev. Isaac (Jr.):2, 12, 16, 25, 27, 30, 33, 40, 43, 54, 56, 62, 68, 70. [Two-Seed-In-The-Spirit Baptist. He was son of Rev. Isaac Denton, Sr., & wife Rebecca Ethridge, & was b. Dec. 23, 1806, Clinton Co., Ky.; d. Warren Co., Tenn., Apr. 7, 1889; interred, Concord Baptist Church, nr. McMinnville, Tenn., where he was the minister for almost 40 yrs. This group has been called many names: "Primitive Baptist", "Hardshell Baptist", & "Two-Seed-In-The-Spirit Baptist". Edythe Whitley, SOME OF THE DESCENDANTS OF REV. RICHARD DENTON, McMinnville, Tenn., Womack Printing Co., 1959.]

DENTON, Jeremiah. See: Rev. Ozias Denton, below.

DENTON, Rev. Ozias: 14, 19, 25, 26, 30, 31, 47, 50, 51, 55, 56, 61, 68, 73. [He was probably b. in Ky., the son of Jeremiah Denton. Rev. Ozias m.

Susan Walling, & they settled in Ark., before the Civil War. He followed a similar doctrine to that of his first cousin, Rev. Isaac Denton..."Two-Seed-In-The-Spirit..".]

DENTON, Rebecca (Ethridge). See: Rev. Isaac Denton, Jr.

DENTON, REV. RICHARD, SOME OF THE DESCENDANTS OF. See: Rev. Isaac Denton

DENTON, Rev. Tidence L.: 20

DIBRELL, M. C., Esq.: 5, 6, 9, 12, 13, 19, 20, 24, 25, 31, 34, 37, 38, 41, 44, 50, 51, 53, 55, 60, 63, 66, 68, 71

DILDINE, Rev. Hezekiah. [Was b. Apr. 11, 1793; d. Aug. 11, 1882; buried at Wesley's Chapel. On May 26, 1846, he gave to "the Methodist Episcopal Church" land on Taylor's Creek, including Mt. Zion meeting house. No trace has been found of the Mt. Zion Church. Dildine is also credited with giving the land for Wesley's Chapel.]

DODSON, Jesse: 18

DODSON, John: 18. [Revol. soldier.]

DODSON, Solomon: 17

DOLIANTE, J. Sharon J.: vii

DOLIANTE, William John: vii

DOLIANTE, Mrs. Wm. J.: vii

DOYLE, Adelphia: 68

DUNCAN, John J., Esq.: 4, 8, 22, 53, 73'

EASTLAND, Chas. S., Esq.: 7, 16, 33

EICHBAUM, Rev. J.: 61

ELKINS, John G.: 34

ELLIS, Rev. John A.: 40

ELLIS, Rev. J. J. [He was appointed to the pastorate of the congregation of the Sparta Methodist Church in 1852, and apparently left in 1853. It is assumed that Rev. J.J. Ellis of the church register, is the same as the Rev. John A. Ellis, who performed the marriage of Jefferson Leftwich & Luraney C. Lisk, on Aug. 30, 1854. Members of the Leftwich family were parishioners of the Methodist church in Sparta.]

FANCHER, Mary: vi

FARRELL, Rev. B. F.: 19, 65

FISKE, Moses. See: Rev. Thos. McBride

FLOYD GRAVEYARD. See: Rev. Ri. Simpson

FORD, Rev. Abraham: 46
FOREST, Rev. R. A.: 2, 67
FRASIER, FRASURE, Richmond, Esq.: 40, 73
FROST, Elijah, Esq.: 4, 15, 51, 66, 74
FRUYSHURD, Rev. David: 35
FRYER, Mary: iii, 9, 28, 63
GENEALOGICAL SERENDIPITY, Vol. I: iii, v, vi
GHONNLEY, Rev. W. G.: 31
GILL, John: 40
GILLENTINE, Jane (___). See: Rev. Jesse E. Hickman
GILLENTINE, John, Esq.: 9, 10, 13, 14, 17, 23, 32, 40, 43, 44, 57, 59, 62, 72
GILLENTINE, Nicholas. See: Rev. Jesse E. Hickman
GILLENTINE, Susan J. See: Rev. Jesse E. Hickman
GIST, Joseph, Esq.: 10, 29, 33, 36, 50, 60, 69
GLENN, Joseph W., Esq.: 3, 44, 61, 66, 71
GLENN, Wm., Esq.: 10, 24, 30, 32, 34, 35, 45, 46, 48, 63, 68, 70, 71
GLENN, Wm., Jr., Esq.: 37
GOODMAN(?), Rev. Wm.: 11
GOODWIN GRAVEYARD. See: Rev. Dempsey M. Southard
GOODWIN, Rev. Wm.: 9, 11, 15, 25, 26, 53, 58, 66, 73. [He came to White Co., from Smith Co. Preached at "Old" Macedonia, nr. Baker's Cross Roads. Left during the Civil War. Buried nr. Shelbyville, Tenn.]
GRACY, Hugh, Esq.: 64
GRAHAM, Andrew, Esq.: 5, 8, 10, 28, 56, 59, 64, 68, 69
GRAHAM, Rev. Chas.: 10
GRAHAM, I.(J.?) H., Esq.: 34, 47
GREEN, Avery: 34
GREEN, Delilah (Stype): 14
GREEN(E), Rev. John: vii, 14, 18, 38, 41, 53, 57, 58. [Baptist.]
GREEN, Mary (Fryer): 9, 28, 63
GREEN, Nancy Judith: iii
GREEN, Thos., Esq.: 3, 5, 6, 11, 14, 20, 22, 25, 27, 29, 30, 31, 37, 55, 59, 62, 65, 66, 68, 74. [Son of Rev. John.]
GREEN(E), Wm., Esq.: iii, 9, 25, 27, 28, 63. [Son of Rev. John.]
GRISHAM, GRISSOM, John L., Esq.: 6, 14,

15, 16, 22, 25, 34, 49, 52, 61, 63, 65, 72, 73
HAISLIP, Calvin W. H. See: Rev. W. C. Haislip
HAISLIP, Rev. W. C.: 8, 58. [This might be the Rev. Hazelett that joined the Sparta Congregation of the Methodist Church in 1853, & presumably left that body in 1853. Yet his marriage of Hosea Broyles and Elizabeth Sperry on Jan. 1, 1857, indicates that he still had some connection with that congregation. *Note: We don't think the surname Haislip should be confused with Hazelett. This compiler's distant cousin & grt. aunt, Mary Jane (Young) Scoggin, m. (2) Nov. 2, 1870, Hempstead Co., Ark., Calvin W.H. Haislip...possible son or other relative of the Rev. W. C. Haislip. sjd]*
HALE, Rev. Elijah: 70
HARPENDING, John W., Esq.: 61
HAYES, Jas. T., Esq.: 27, 28, 55
HAZELETT, Rev. See: Rev. W.C. Haislip
HERD, Rev. James: 2, 5, 14, 18, 24, 27, 30, 31, 36, 40, 42, 45, 47, 48, 49, 55, 64, 65, 73, 74
HICKMAN, Benjamin. See: Rev. Jesse E. Hickman
HICKMAN, Rev. Francis M[arion?]: 27, 32, 63
HICKMAN, Rev. Jesse Everett: 3, 4, 8, 10, 11, 12, 13, 14, 15, 16, 25, 26, 28, 32, 36, 37, 42, 44, 47, 48, 50, 52, 54, 59, 62, 71, 73, 74, 75. [He was the son of Benjamin & Judith Hickman, b. Oct. 22, 1805; d. Dec. 26, 1888, White Co. He m. Susan J. Gillentine, dau. of Nicholas & Jane Gillentine. They are interred at the Weaver-Hickman Graveyard on Cherry Creek, in White Co. Rev. Hickman was minister of the Cherry Creek Presbyterian Church for almost 40 years.]
HICKMAN, Judith (___). See: Rev. Jesse E. Hickman
HITCHCOCK, B., Esq.: 12
HITCHCOCK, Robt., Esq.: 1, 4, 5, 8, 16, 17, 20, 26, 29, 31, 39, 41, 43, 48,

49, 52, 54, 56, 58

HITCHCOCK, Zachariah, Esq.: 14, 29, 30, 31

HOOKER, Rev. W. H.: 18, 73

HORDE, Rev. Jesse. [He was appointed to the Sparta congregation of the Methodist Church in 1834. He was followed in 1842 by the Rev. S.S. Yarbrough.]

HORNE, Thos., J.P.: 58

HOWARD, Geo. D., J.P.: 61

HUDDLESTON, Rev. W. B.: 11

HUDGENS, Wm., Esq.: 3, 6, 29, 45

HUNTER, Joseph: 42

HUTCHINGS, Chas.: 20

HUTCHINS, William. [He was listed in the 1850 Census, Dist. 13, White Co., as "M.G.O.S.P." He was b. 1822, in Pennsylvania.]

HUTSON, Rev. Abel: 15, 22, 27, 34, 40, 47, 56, 66. [A Methodist minister, he d. in 1845; buried nr. Mt. Pisgah.]

HUTSON, Abel C.: 40

HUTSON, Geo.: 47

HUTSON, Matthias, Esq.: 2, 31, 60

HUTSON, Rev. Thos. E.: 5, 12, 13, 14, 15, 16, 17, 22, 27, 32, 34, 35, 37, 38, 39, 40, 41, 45, 50, 55, 56, 62, 65, 69, 72, 73. [A Methodist minister, buried Mt. Pisgah Cemetery.]

HYDER, Joseph D., Esq.: 8, 18, 42, 52, 59, 70, 73

ILLINOIS, HISTORY OF MENARD AND MASON COUNTIES: 27

IRVIN, James H., Esq.: 22

ISHAM, James. See: Rev. Phillip Mulkey

ISOM, Jas. H., Esq.: 12, 21, 63

JACKSON, James, Esq.: 2, 32, 60, 62, 64

JAMES, Rev. J. J.: 22, 50, 55

JARED, Elizabeth (Raulsten). See: Rev. Wm. Jared

JARED, Rev. Wm.: 7, 8, 13, 14, 17, 18, 19, 24, 25, 26, 27, 28, 33, 35, 36, 38, 43, 47, 48, 49, 51, 53, 54, 60, 63, 65, 67. [He was the son of Wm. & Elizabeth (Raulsten) Jared; born June 18, 1805; d. nr. Sparta, Sept. 30, 1861. He was a Methodist minister in the days of the Circuit riders. On Nov. 8, 1850, he was designated as a trustee of the First

Methodist Church in Sparta, yet his name does not appear on the church rolls. He m. Dec. 13, 1837, Martha Phillips "Patsy" Jett, dau. of John and Mary (White) Jett; grd-dau. of John & Martha (Phillips) White, Sr. Mrs. Jared was a member of the First Methodist Church for almost 50 years, her death occurring in July, 1891. The Jareds were buried in the old City Cemetery, Sparta.]

JARVIS, Levi, Esq.: 24, 25, 29, 50, 56, 57, 58

JETT, John, Esq.: 69; also see: Rev. Wm. Jared

JETT, Martha Phillips "Patsy". See: Rev. Wm. Jared

JETT, Mary (White). See: Rev. Wm. Jared

JOHNSON'S CHAPEL (Baptist). See: Rev. Henry B. Johnson

JOHNSON, Rev. Henry B.: 47. [He was b. Aug. 18, 1818; d. June 16, 1903; m. Aug. 4, 1841, to Henrietta Lollar. He was a Baptist minister in the Calfkiller section of present day Putnam County. Buried, Johnson's Chapel.]

JOHNSON, Wm. C., Esq.: 5, 6, 7, 10, 11, 19, 20, 21, 23, 33, 40, 43, 54, 59, 62, 64, 69, 71, 72, 74

JONES, Rev. Irvin: 6, 58

JONES, Rev. John A.: 28, 30, 49

JONES, Thos., Esq.: 1, 4, 10, 17, 20, 26, 34, 36, 38, 49, 57, 67, 75

JUDD, Rev. Nathan: 13, 36, 50

JULIEN, Rev. John: 1, 64

KELLEY, Rev. John. [Minister of the First Methodist Church in Sparta, in 1825...to c.1834. He returned to the Sparta congregation in 1847, but is not located in the 1850 census.]

KILGROW, E. W.: 42

KING, Rev. Elias: 54

KNOWLES, James A., Esq.: 10, 12, 13, 14, 21, 26, 27, 30, 33, 34, 35, 40, 46, 51, 55, 59, 61, 63, 71, 72

KNOWLES, Wm., Esq.: 10, 11, 24, 28, 36, 39, 60, 67, 69

KUYKENDALL, Rev. Peter: 58

LANE, Jonathan P.: 34

LANE, Martha (Anderson): 40

LANE, Turner, Sr.: 40. [Revol. soldier.
His Pension Record shows he was b.
Jan. 9, 1762, Hanover Co., Va.; &
his m. to Martha Anderson, Sept.
27, 1787, is on record, Washington
Co., Va.]
LANSDEN, Rev. James King: 54. [He was
b. Mar. 31, 1803; d. Jan. 14, 1877.
He m. (1) Judith McDonald; m. (2)
Jane Sidney Simpson. The Rev. Lan-
sden & his (2) wife are buried at
Old Zion Presbyterian Church where
he was minister. He taught school
at Taylor's Creek, at a place later
known as The Lansden House. This
property was later sold, & is today
(1976) occupied by the Lansden
Church of Christ.]
LANSDEN, Rev. John M:2.[He was son of
Rev. Jas. King Lansden.]
LARGE, Rev. William. [He was appointed
to the pastorate of the Sparta
Methodist congregation in 1857, and
apparently left in the same year.
On Oct. 6, 1859, he m. Saraphina
Snodgrass, the dau. of James and
Margaret (McKinney) Snodgrass, of
Sparta. Mrs. Large d. on Jan. 11,
1865, at Sulphur Springs, Smith
Co., Tenn.]
LASITER, LASSATER, Rev. Daniel: 41, 42
LAWRENCE, Rev. A. F.: 39, 55. [He was
appointed pastor of the Methodist
congregation in 1851, where it ap-
pears that he remained for one year.
In Mar., 1853, & Apr., 1854, he per-
formed two marriages in White Co.]
LEFTWICH, Jefferson. See: Rev. J.J.
Ellis
LENDON, Benjamin F. ["The Rev. Benjamin
F. Lendon will preach at the court-
house in Sparta on the 4th day of
August." Aug. 3, 1825. SPARTA RE-
VIEW.]
LENTZ, Rev. G. W.: 6, 7
LEONARD, Charles: v, vi, vii
LISK, Luraney C. See: Rev. J. J. Ellis
LITTLE, F. S., Esq.: 21, 22
LITTLE, Wm., Esq.: 15, 18, 33, 42, 50,
51, 53, 63
LOLLAR, Corder: 38
LOLLAR, Henrietta. See: Rev. Henry B.

Johnson
LOLLAR, Isaac, Esq.: 15, 70
LOWERY(REY), Jas. B., Esq.: 19, 34, 46,
74
LYDA, Henry J., Esq.: 1, 21, 39, 41
LYDA, Rhody: vi
LYLES, J. B.: 69
LYLES, Rev. Stephen B.: 37, 45, 69
MCBRIDE, Rev. Andrew: 11, 50
MCBRIDE, Rev. Thomas. [On Nov. 1, 1813,
Moses Fiske gave to "a Christian
Society" under the Pastoral care of
Rev. Thomas McBride, land to in-
clude "the graveyard near the old
meeting house", at Plum Creek. This
is assumed to be a Presbyterian
congregation, & as such is one of
the oldest churches in the northern
section of White Co.]
MCCONNELL, Rev. Miles Washington: 3, 8,
11, 24, 25, 26, 27, 30, 33, 36, 44,
56, 59. [A Presbyterian minister,
he was b. Apr. 25, 1810; d. Dec. 4,
1899; buried, Old Zion Presbyterian
Church.]
MCDONALD, Judith. See: Rev. Jas. K.
Lansden
MCGUIRE, Rev. C.: 58
MCMANN(?), Robt. H.: 47
MCMANUS, Robt. H.: 2, 9, 10, 13, 20, 28,
29, 34, 41, 44, 46, 50, 57, 66
MADEWELL, John, Esq.: 7, 19, 33, 35, 46,
55, 64, 70
MANN, Rev. John Henry: 12, 18, 53, 62.
[Methodist.]
MANUS, John P.: 5
MARTIN, Rev. G. W.: 12, 17
MARTIN, Rev. Wm.: 7, 18, 58, 64, 67, 70
MASON, Joshua, Esq.: 24, 42
MENEFEE, Joseph S., Esq.: 1
MERSLOM, J. W., Esq.: 46
METHODIST CHURCH, FIRST. See: Rev's.
Wm. Jared, John Kelley
METHODIST CHURCH, MT. PISGAH. See: Rev's
Peter Burum, Abel Hutson, Thos.
Hutson, Elisha Webb, Jeremiah Webb.
METHODIST CHURCH, SPARTA. See: Rev's.
S.H. Brown, ___ Corbin, J.J. Ellis,
W.C. Haislip, Jesse Horde, Wm.
Large, F.S. Petway, Jas. H. Richey,
Berry M. Stephens, S.S. Yarbrough.]
M. E. Church. See: Rev. A.G. Copeland
-99-

MITCHELL, Mrs. B. K.: vi
MITCHELL, Rev. David L.: 39
MITCHELL, John W., Esq.: 11, 16, 17, 18,
47, 53, 58, 59, 60, 70, 73, 74, 75
MITCHELL, Joseph G., Esq.: 2, 15, 16,
18, 41, 42, 46, 57, 63, 74
MITCHELL, Nancy: 42, 49, 70
MOORE, Rev. Patrick: 56
MOORE, Samuel: 61
MOORE, Wm. W., Esq.: 12, 18, 41, 49, 51
MORGAN, Rev. James H.: 1, 2, 4, 15, 16,
18, 27, 28, 30, 31, 35, 38, 41, 45,
54, 55, 61, 67, 69, 70, 73, 74
MOSS, Rev. Arnold: 12, 23, 25, 31, 33,
40, 44, 45, 49, 53, 57, 65, 66, 68,
73
MT. ZION MEETING HOUSE. See: Rev. Hez-
ekiah Dildine
MUERSHON, Joab W., Esq.: 19
MULKEY, Rev. Phillip. ["The Rev. Phill-
ip Mulkey, will preach a Funeral
Sermon, at the courthouse in Sparta
Friday the 23d of July--and on the
day following, at the residence of
James Isham, decd." SPARTA REVIEW,
Wed. June 30, 1824.]
MURPHEY, Rev. N. L.: 42
N.S.D.A.R. Records: 27, 29
NASHVILLE NEWS, THE (ARKANSAS): 45
NEILE, Henry, J.P.: 41
"OLD MACEDONIA". See: Rev. Wm. Goodwin
OLIVER, Alexander, Esq.: 2, 53, 60
PENDERGRASS, Rev. T. W.: 60
PENNINGTON, John, Esq.: 4, 8, 20, 21,
49, 50, 52, 54, 55, 71
PERKINS CEMETERY. See: Rev. Levi Per-
kins
PE(I)RKINS, Rev. Levi: 1, 3, 6, 7, 9,
10, 15, 16, 18, 19, 26, 30, 32, 33,
35, 37, 38, 39, 41, 42, 46, 48, 49,
52, 54, 65, 66, 72. [He was a Bap-
tist minister; buried at the Per-
kins Cemetery in present-day Put-
nam County.]
PETWAY, Rev. F. S. [He was appointed to
the pastorate of the Sparta Methodist congregation in 1855, & returned there in 1857.]
PHILLIPS, Martha: 70
PLEASANT GROVE MEETING HOUSE & CAMP
GROUND (Methodist). See: Rev.
Joseph B. Wynns

POINTER (or PONITER?), Rev. John B.: 4,
33, 44, 57, 59
PRESBYTERIAN CHURCH, CHERRY CREEK. See:
Rev. Jesse E. Hickman
PRESBYTERIAN CHURCH, OLD ZION. See:
Rev's. Jas. K. Lansdan, Miles W.
McConnell
PRESBYTERIAN CHURCH, PLUM CREEK. See:
Rev. Thos. McBride
PRICE, Shadrach, Esq.: 4, 15, 22, 33,
41, 43, 50, 54, 57, 60
PUCKETT, John: vi
RICE, Rev. Jesse G.: 37
RICHEY (or RITCHEY), Rev. James H.: 5,
15, 22, 49, 63. [He was b. in 1827
in Tenn.; m. Feb. 7, 1854, by the
Rev. A. F. Lawrence, to Elizabeth
Snodgrass, dau. of James & Margaret
(McKinney) Snodgrass. He was prob-
ably a Methodist, as several mem-
bers of his wife's family attended
the Sparta Methodist Church. Eliz-
abeth's sister Saraphina m. the
Rev. William Large. Elizabeth Snod-
grass Richey d. July 27, 1871, in
Waco, Texas.]
RITCHIE, Robert R. [Listed in 1850 Cen-
sus, 6th Dist., White Co., as
"M.G.C.P.", or Minister of the Gos-
pel, Cumberland Presbyterian. He
was b. in 1812, in Tenn.]
RI(T)CHEY, Rev. R. R.(as above): 7, 29,
45, 46, 55, 64, 65
RI(T)CHEY, Rev. V. V.: 34
ROGERS, Anderson S., Esq.: 3, 6, 13, 15,
18, 23, 27, 28, 30, 31, 33, 41, 48,
49, 57, 68, 74
ROSE, Wm. W.: 73
RUSSELL, Wm. I.(or P.), Esq.: 1, 16, 34,
35, 37, 39, 41, 53, 55, 64, 67
SAVAGE, Kenall: 35
SAYLORS, Abraham (or Abram), Esq.: 6, 9,
20, 21, 31, 32, 37, 42, 63, 71, 73.
[He was a Methodist minister.]
SCARBORO, Elisha: 5
SCOGGIN, Elizabeth (White): 40, 45, 68
SCOGGIN, Hannah: 72
SCOGGINS, Jesse, Esq.: 40
SCOGGIN, Rev. John, Jr.: v, vii, 40, 45,
58, 68
SCOGGIN, Mary Jane (Young). See: Rev.
W. C. Haislip

-100-

SEWELL, Jesse S.: 6, 21. [He was listed in the 1850 Census, Dist. 12, White Co., as "M.G.C.C."; probably lived in the vicinity of Yankeetown. He was b. in Ky., in 1815.]
SHAW, A. L. Esq.: 1, 64
SIMMONS, Rev. James: 1, 8
SIMPSON, Jane Sidney. See: Rev. James K. Lansden
SIMPSON, Rev. Richard: 19, 24, 29, 30, 57, 67, 70. [He was a Presbyterian minister; b. Nov. 24, 1811, in Va.; d. Aug. 2, 1889, with interment in the Floyd Graveyard, Big Spring Community, White Co., Tenn.]
SIMS, Andrew J., Esq.: 10, 21, 29, 35, 42, 60, 63
SIMS, O. H. P., Esq.: 23, 24
SMITH, Rev. E. A.: 47
SMITH, John, Esq.: 56
SNODGRASS, David L., Esq.: 2, 4, 5, 7, 8, 11, 14, 15, 16, 18, 19, 23, 25, 27, 29, 31, 33, 36, 38, 39, 40, 41, 42, 43, 44, 46, 49, 50, 51, 54, 60, 61, 63, 64, 65, 67, 71, 72, 73, 74
SNODGRASS, Elizabeth. See: Rev. James H. Richey
SNODGRASS, James. See: Rev's. Wm. Large, James H. Richey
SNODGRASS, Margaret (McKinney). See: Rev's. Wm. Large, Jas. H. Richey
SNODGRASS, Saraphina. See: Rev. William Large & Rev. Jas. H. Richey
SOUTHARD, Dempsey M., Esq.: 20, 32, 44, 57, 60. [He was a Methodist minister. He was b. Sept. 24, 1819, a son of Micajah Southard; d. Apr. 22, 1883; buried at the Goodwin Graveyard, in White Co.]
SOUTHARD, Micajah. See: Rev. Dempsey M. Southard, immediately above.
SPARTA REVIEW. See: Rev's. Isaac Anderson, Benj. F. Lendon, Phillip Mulkey, Mr. Watson
SPARTONIAN AND MT. DISTRICT ADVERTISER: 40
SPERRY, Elizabeth. See: Rev. W.C. Haislip
SPERRY, Thos. L.: 9
STEPHENS, Rev. Berry M. [He served as minister of the Sparta Methodist congregation in 1859, & again be-

tween 1866 & 1869. As B. M. Stevens he performed a marriage in White Co. in 1852. On Jan. 21, 1856 he was living at Cornersville, Tenn. He m. Sophronia Turney, dau. of Samuel & Caroline (Fiske) Turney of Sparta. Rev. & Mrs. Stephens moved to Texas, where it is believed they settled nr. Clarendon.]
STEPHENS, J. C., Esq.: 1
STEVENS, B. M.: 15
STEVENS, John C., Esq.: 20, 22
STONE, Rev. Amos M.: 23, 74
STONE, Rev. Corder: 8, 11, 35, 49, 51, 64
STONE, Rev. J. H.: 19
STONE, Thomas, "Elder": 9
STONE, Rev. Thos.: 1, 5, 6, 7, 8, 9, 10, 11, 12, 15, 16, 20, 21, 29, 30, 32, 33, 34, 36, 38, 40, 42, 48, 50, 51, 52, 54, 55, 61, 64, 71, 72. [He was listed in the 1850 Census, Dist. 10, White Co., as a farmer & "MGCC". His tombstone, at Stone's Seminary Free Will Baptist Church, Putnam Co., Tenn., reads:"Rev. Thos. Stone Dec. 24, 1806 - Oct. 29, 1873".]
STUBBLEFIELD, Rev. Geo.: 62 (Baptist)
STYPE, Delilah: 14
SULLIVAN, Jesse M., Esq.: 3, 20, 25, 34, 37, 60, 63
SULLIVENT, C.: 11
SUMMAR, Rev. S. L.: 70
SWINDLE, John, Esq.: 20, 29, 39, 44, 64, 66, 68
TARRANT, Rev. J. W.: 39
TATE, Sallie (Whiteside): 72
TATE, Vincent B.: 72
TAYLOR, Creed A., Esq.: 1, 3, 4, 11, 24, 27, 28, 30, 36, 39, 43, 45, 46, 59, 69
TEMPLETON, John A., Esq.: 5, 59, 61, 71, 72
TOWNSEND, Andrew, J.P.: 51
TUCKER, Wm. R., Esq.: 1, 7, 11, 16, 19, 32, 38, 41, 47, 57, 61, 67, 68, 73
TURNEY, Caroline (Fiske). See: Rev. Berry M. Stephens
TURNEY, Samuel. See: Rev. Berry M. Stephens
TURNEY, Sophronia. See: Rev. Berry M. Stephens

US(S)REY, Samuel, Esq.: 21, 26, 42, 68, 71
WALLING, Jesse, Esq.: 13, 17, 20, 37, 56, 57, 68
WALLING, John, Esq.: 63
WALLING, Susan. See: Rev. Isaac Denton
WATSON, Rev. Mr. [MASONIC-"By request of the Fraternity of this place, the Rev. Mr. Watson will preach a Sermon at the Court House in Sparta on the 27th inst. Citizens and others are respectfully invited to attend." Dec. 22, 1824. SPARTA REVIEW.]
WEAVER-HICKMAN GRAVEYARD. See: Rev. Jesse E. Hickman
WEBB, Rev. Elisha: 14. [Buried Mt. Pisgah]
WEBB, James, Esq.: 39, 67
WEBB, Rev. Jeremiah: 9, 35, 46. [He's buried at Mt. Pisgah.]
WEBB, W., Esq.: 56
WESLEY'S CHAPEL (Methodist Church). See: Rev. Hezekiah Dildine
WHALEY, Rev. John: 9, 65
WHITE, Adelphia (Doyle): 68
WHITE, Dyer P[hillips]: 70
WHITE, Elizabeth: 40, 45
WHITE, Hugh Lawson: v
WHITE, John, Jr.: 68, 70
WHITE, John, Sr. (Revolutionary soldier) :v, 70, also see: Rev. Wm. Jared
WHITE, Martha (Phillips). See: Rev. Wm. Jared
WHITE, Nancy (Mitchell): 42, 49, 70
WHITE, Woodson P.: v, 42, 49, 70
WHITESIDE, Sallie B.: 72
WHITLEY, Edythe. See: Rev. Isaac Denton
WHITLEY, Joel, Esq.: 17, 20, 41, 42, 43, 46, 52, 57

WIL(L)HITE, John, Esq.: 5, 10, 12, 19, 21, 22, 29, 33, 34, 35, 40, 47, 53, 56, 67, 71
WILLIAMS, James: v, 72
WILLIAMS, Rev. Josiah: 4, 10, 32
WILLIAMS, Sampson: v
WILSON, Wm., Esq.: 3, 6, 15, 24, 43, 46, 59, 74
WISDOM, Wm.: 9
WOODS, Waman L., Esq.: 2, 5, 16, 55, 72
WOODS, Wm.: 66
WOOD(W)ARD, Rev. Isaac C.: 22, 36, 37, 39, 40, 53, 67. (Methodist)
WYNN(ES), Rev. Joseph B.: 13, 24, 38, 40, 42, 66. [He was a Methodist minister, but congregation undetermined. On Nov. 8, 1850, he was termed a trustee of the Methodist Church in Sparta, as was the Rev. William Jared, neither of whom appear on the official church rolls. On Aug. 29, 1853, he was a trustee of the Pleasant Grove Meeting House and Camp Ground, for the M. E. Church, probably located in present day Putnam County.]
YARBROUGH, Rev. S. S.: 17, 22, also see: Rev. Jesse Horde. [He was a Methodist minister for the Sparta congregation. Church records indicate he was pastor there from 1842 to 1847. He was certainly at that church in Jan. 1842 & Mar. 1843, when he performed marriages.]
YATES, Rev. John: 6, 7, 12, 23
YEAGER, Solomon, J.P. (Esq.): 7, 9, 16, 22, 33, 35, 44, 51, 54, 69, 73